Mousehole the Cornish Jewel - 3rd Edition

In this 3rd edition of my Mousehole book we will go on a pictorial and descriptive journey through the history and splendour of the Cornish fishing village of Mousehole. The village cascades down the steep hillside to its picturesque harbour. People have watched the boats come in and out of the harbour for centuries. We will then go on an exploration, further afield, to many of the gardens, places and visitor attractions that make Cornwall such a great and vibrant place to visit. I really do believe that Mousehole is the jewel in the crown of Cornwall…

by Norfolk Watercolour Artist - Alan R. Massen
Published in Great Britain by Rainbow Publications UK

First Published in 2016 by Rainbow Publications UK
2nd Edition Published in 2019 by Rainbow Publications UK
3rd Edition Published in 2020 by Rainbow Publications UK

Copyright © 2019 Alan R. Massen

The moral right of Alan R. Massen to be identified as the author of this work has been asserted in accordance with the UK Copyright, Designs and Patents. Act of 1988. All rights reserved. No part of this book may be reproduced, or stored in a retrieval system, or transmitted in any form or by any means, electronic, mechanical, photocopying, recording, or otherwise, without the prior written permission of both the author and the above publisher of this book All imagery and illustrations .

© Alan R. Massen

Neither the publisher nor the author can accept liability for the use of any of the materials, methods or information recommended in this book or for any consequences arising out of their use, nor can they be held responsible for any errors or omissions that may be found in the text or may occur at a future date as a result of changes in rules, laws or equipment All manufacturers, sellers, product names and services identified in this book are used in editorial fashion and for the benefit of such companies with no intention of any infringement of trademarks. No such use or the use of any trade name is intended to convey endorsement or other affiliation with this book. Every effort has been made to obtain the necessary permissions with reference to copyright material, both illustrative and quoted. We apologize for any omissions in this respect and will be pleased to make the appropriate acknowledgements in any future edition.

Paperback Edition ISBN 978-0-9935591-1-2
Typeset in Minion Pro

Published in Great Britain by Rainbow Publications UK

About the Author

Alan was born in the city of Norwich in the county of Norfolk, England in November 1949. When Alan was still a teenager he started painting whilst attending art classes in Norwich. In his mid-teens he had two paintings accepted for a National Art Exhibition held in London and other major UK cities. Alan spent most of his working life as a professional Health and Safety Advisor and rarely picked up a paint brush until Alan, his wife Susie and daughter Ginny (his other daughter Mandy is married and lives with her husband Adrian in Sheffield) moved out of the city of Norwich into the countryside in 1993. They moved to a little village called East Lexham in the heart of Norfolk. The village was very peaceful and pretty. This helped inspire Alan to take up watercolour painting once again. In 2004 they moved to another small West Norfolk village near Downham Market where they still live today. In 2008 Alan had to retire due to ill health (bad knees) and whilst he still painted regularly he began to spend more and more time gardening. In 2013 his wife Susie suggested that he kept a gardening diary to record his adventures in the garden and capture the changing seasons, animals, birds and the successes and failures of being a gardener he encountered. By the following year Susie suggested that he should write a book from his diary and include illustrations of both the garden and his artwork.

In 2014 Alan's first book was published by Creative Gateway called **"Retiring to the Garden – Year One".** This proved such a success that Alan decided to follow this up with his second book called **"Retiring into a Rainbow"** featuring his watercolour paintings. He then in 2015 published **"Retiring to Our Garden – Year Two"** published this time by Rainbow Publications UK. He then re-issued his first two books this time in a **"Second Edition"**. Also published by Rainbow Publications UK. From 2016 to 2018 he published: **"Skiathos a Greek Island Paradise", "Norfolk the County of my Birth", "Art Inspired by a Rainbow", "Ibiza Island of Dreams", "Majorca Island in the Sun", "Flip-flops and Shades on Thassos"** and finally **"Mardle and a Troshin' in Norfolk"**. In 2019 and 2020 he started on the following new editions of his books entitled: **"England the Country of my Birth", "Mousehole the Cornish Jewel", "Sunshine and Shades on Kefalonia", "Shades and Flip-flops on Zakynthos", "Crete and the Island of Santorini", "Cyprus the Pyramids and the Holy Land", "Corfu and Mainland Greece" ", "Trips into my Mind's Eye"** and finally **"Flip-flops and Shades on many Greek Islands".** When completed they will also be published by Rainbow Publications UK.

Susie and Alan…

Books by the same Author

Retiring to the Garden Year 1 - Paperback
Retiring into a Rainbow - Paperback and Hardback
Retiring into a Rainbow - 1st Edition - My Favourite Artwork 2020 - 1st Edition
Retiring to our Garden Year one - 1st & 2nd Editions
Retiring to our Garden Year two - 1st & 2nd & 3rd Editions
Retiring into a Rainbow - 1st & 2nd Editions
Skiathos a Greek Island Paradise - 1st & 2nd & 3rd Editions
Norfolk the County of my Birth - 1st & 2nd & 3rd Editions
Art Inspired by a Rainbow - 1st & 2nd & 3rd & 4th Editions
Ibiza Island of Dreams - 1st & 2nd Editions
Majorca Island in the Sun - 1st & 2nd Editions
Flip-Flops and Shades on Thassos - 1st & 2nd & 3rd Editions
Mardle and a Troshin' in Norfolk - 1st & 2nd Editions
England the Country of my Birth - 1st & 2nd Editions
Mousehole the Cornish Jewel - 1st & 2nd & 3rd Editions
Sunshades & Flip-Flops on Kefalonia - 1st & 2nd & 3rd Editions
Shades & Flip-Flops on Zakynthos - 1st & 2nd & 3rd Editions
Trips into my Minds Eye - 1st & 2nd & 3rd & 4th Editions
Corfu and Mainland Greece - 1st & 2nd & 3rd Editions
Crete and the Island of Santorini - 1st & 2nd & 3rd Editions
Cyprus - Pyramids - Holy Land - 1st & 2nd & 3rd Editions
Greek Islands in the Sun - 1st & 2nd & 3rd Editions
Being Greek - 1st & 2nd & 3rd Editions

E-books and Booklets:

Retiring to the Garden Yr 1 - Retiring into a Rainbow - My Art 1997 - 2018 - Skiathos a Greek Paradise Island
My Norfolk - My Greece - My England - My Team - My Skiathos - My Art - My Album of Visual Art
My Village - Greece Land of Gods and Men - Norfolk Wildlife - Civilisation (Empires of the Past)
Boudica Queen of the Iceni - Roman Britain

Alan…

Copyright © 2020 - Alan R. Massen
Published in Great Britain by Rainbow Publications UK.

Books by the same Author

by Norfolk watercolour artist - Alan R. Massen.
Published 1st Edition by Creative Gateway and 2nd Edition by Rainbow Publications UK

Books by the same Author

by Norfolk watercolour artist - Alan R. Massen.
Published in Great Britain by Rainbow Publications UK

Books by the same Author

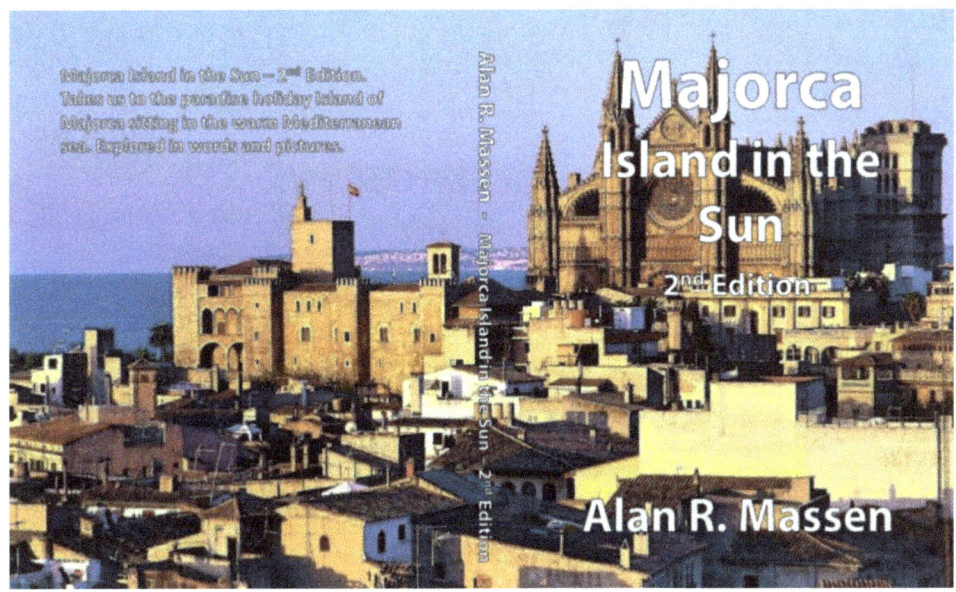

by Norfolk Watercolour Artist Alan R. Massen
Published in Great Britain by Rainbow Publications UK

Books by the same Author

by Norfolk Watercolour Artist - Alan R. Massen
Published in Great Britain by Rainbow Publications UK

Books by the same Author

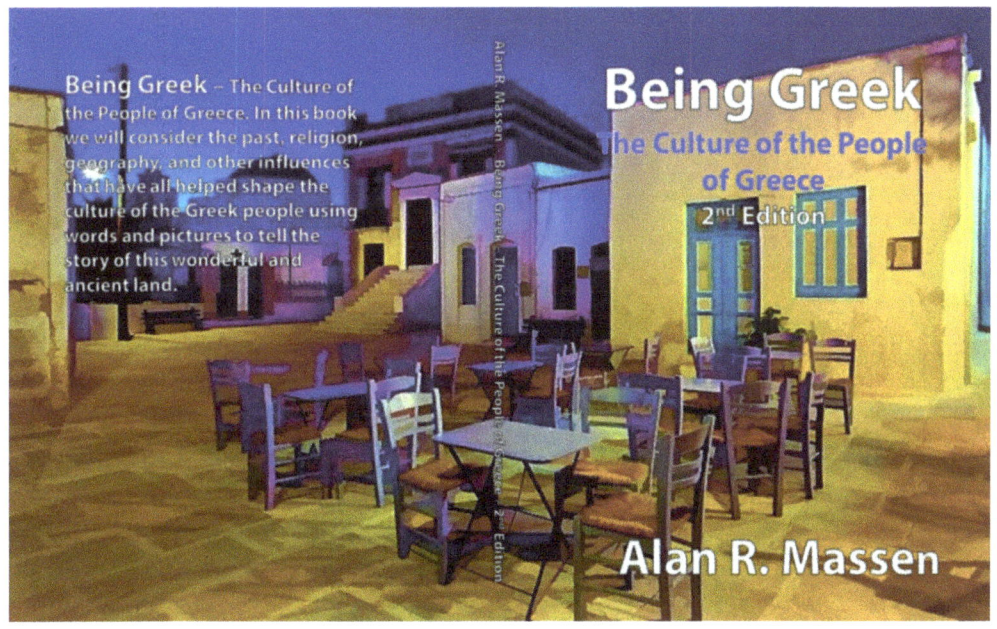

by Norfolk Watercolour Artist - Alan R. Massen
Published in Great Britain by Rainbow Publications UK

Books by the same Author

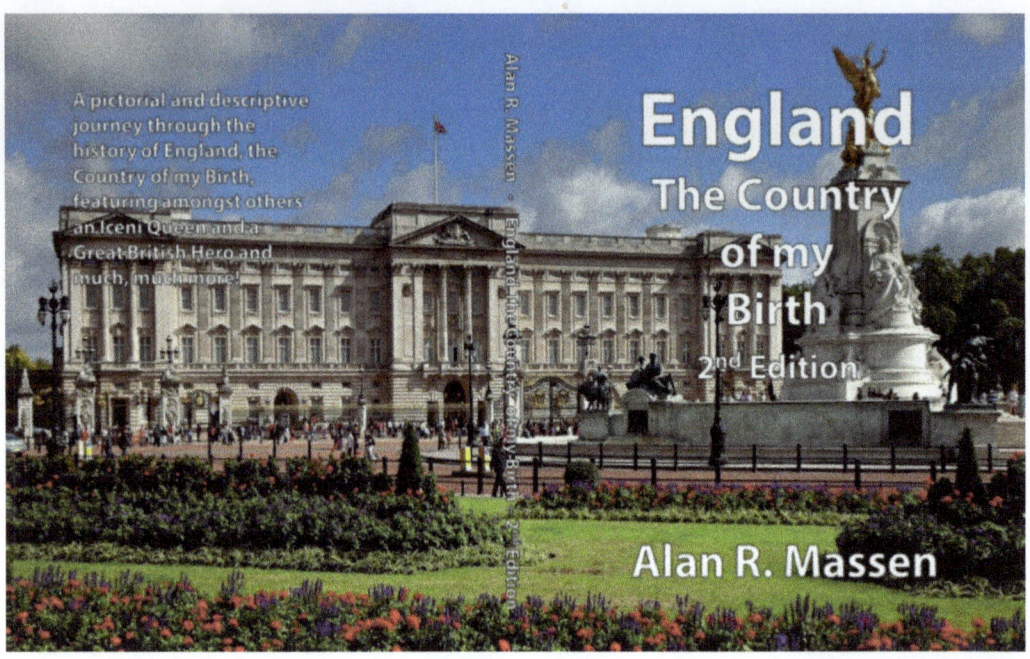

by Norfolk Watercolour Artist - Alan R. Massen
Published in Great Britain by Rainbow Publications UK

Books by the same Author

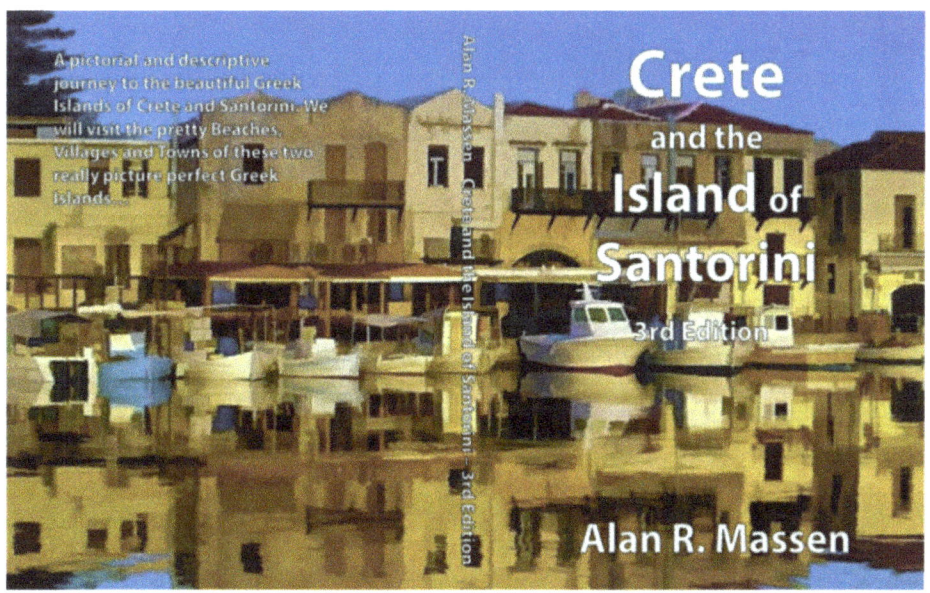

by Norfolk Watercolour Artist - Alan R. Massen
Published in Great Britain by Rainbow Publications UK

Books by the same Author

by Norfolk Watercolour Artist - Alan R. Massen
Published in Great Britain by Rainbow Publications UK

Books by the same Author

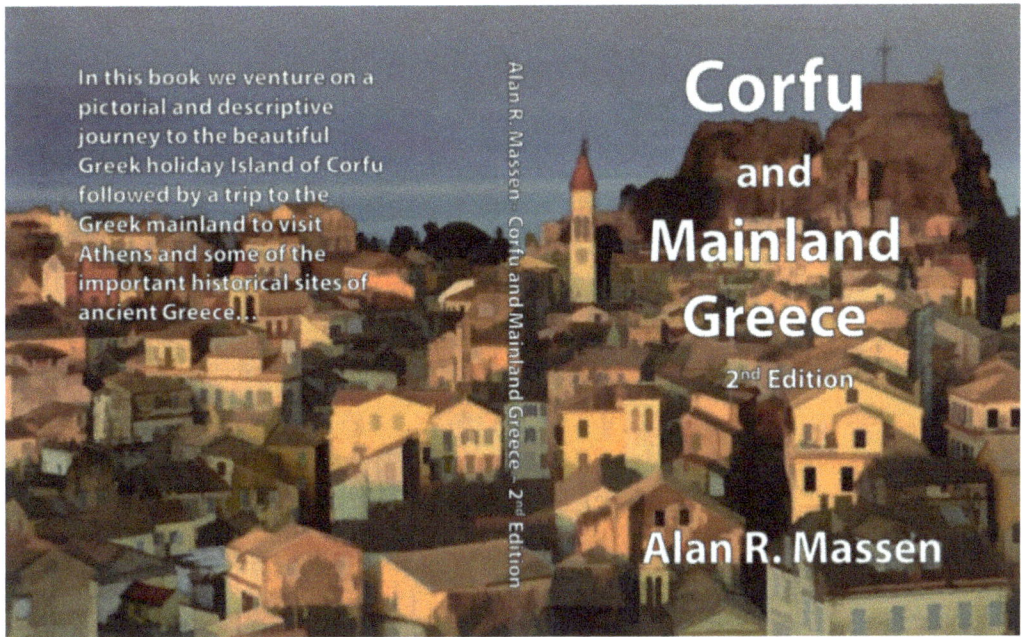

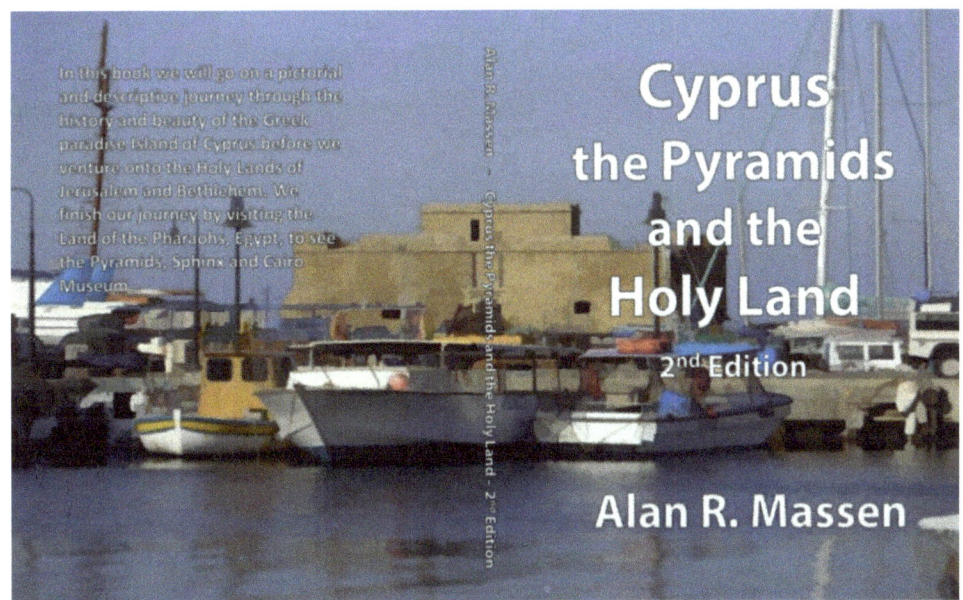

by Norfolk Watercolour Artist - Alan R. Massen
Published in Great Britain by Rainbow Publications UK

Books by the same Author

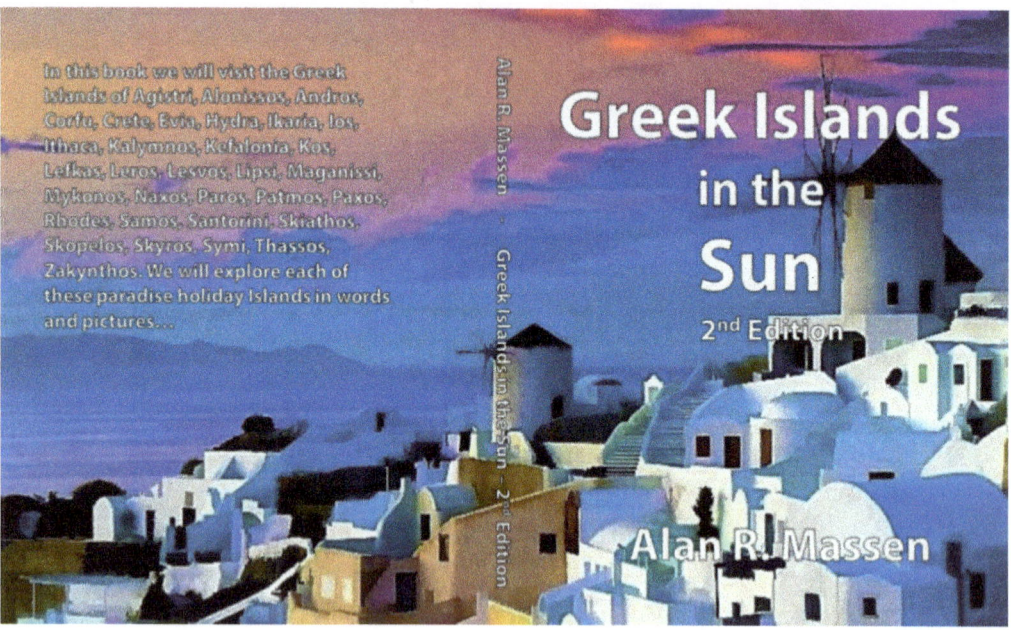

by Norfolk Watercolour Artist - Alan R. Massen
Published in Great Britain by Rainbow Publications UK

Dedication

Welcome to my book called **"Mousehole the Cornish Jewel".** I would like to dedicate this book to all those people worldwide who have lost loved ones during the recent terrible Coronavirus pandemic of 2020. All those who have left us will always be remembered and live on in our hearts and minds as we remember all of the love, support and smiles that they shared with us during their lifetimes. I would also like to thank the wonderful, dedicated and brave doctors, nurses and all of the other essential workers who put their own lives at risk to help others during this tragedy. Their bravery has been an inspiration to us all during this awful time and we thank each and to every one of them. **THANK YOU**…

I would also like to dedicate this book to the loved ones that we have lost and are no longer with us today: my mum Edith, my dad Arthur, my son Paul, Susie's dad Barry, brother Pete and our very good friend Roy. Although sadly they are no longer with us they are not forgotten and the memory of their love and support still inspires me to do better every single day of my life. I would also like to say a big thank you to all of the people that we have met over the years, both at home and abroad. Finally a special mention must also go to my best friend and wife Susie who is always by my side supporting and helping me to enjoy, to the full, everything every day of my life!

Alan…

Susie…

To all of our friends and family I would like to say a big

THANK YOU

Contents

Introduction	1
The History of Mousehole	10
Out and About in Mousehole	26
The Gardens of Cornwall	33
The Castles of Cornwall	47
The Historical Houses of Cornwall	53
The Towns and Villages of Cornwall	65
Exploring Cornwall	155
Our Holiday to Mousehole	169
Mousehole in Colour	194
Acknowledgement	202

Copyright © 2020 Alan R. Massen

Introduction

This book is a pictorial and descriptive journey through the history and splendour of the Cornish fishing village of Mousehole and many of the gardens, castles, houses, villages and towns of Cornwall. The village of Mousehole cascades down the steep hillside to the harbour. People have watched the boats come in and out of its harbour for centuries. This really is the jewel in the crown of Cornwall. In this book you will see numerous examples of my watercolour paintings and photographic artwork to produce the illustrations used throughout this book. I hope you will enjoy exploring Mousehole and Cornwall with me. If you are ready lets begin…

Introduction

Alan, Susie and the harbour in Mousehole…

There are very few places that can be found anywhere in the United Kingdom that have retained their original character and charm in the way that the tiny fishing village of Mousehole in Cornwall has. Susie and I really enjoyed our recent holiday to this small Cornish harbour village nearly on the tip of England. In this book we will go on a visual and text journey to visit the villages history, it's attractions and then take a wander around the village and it's surrounding area based on the last time that we were on holiday there…

Introduction

Mousehole (pronounced "Mowzel") is one of Cornwall's most picturesque villages. It is a stunning collection of yellow-lichened houses, built from the local finely grained Lamorna granite, huddled together around the inner edge of the harbour. Protected from the force of the sea coming across Mounts Bay by two sturdy breakwaters. That said now please come with me to explore this little hidden gem…

Introduction

Alan and Susie on Mousehole harbour beach.

Mousehole is a very attractive tourist holiday destination. It has a small and very safe beach which is located in a sheltered part of the harbour that is very popular with families, particularly those with small children. It is an ideal location for family days out, with safe bathing, quite literally at your feet. So bring your bucket, spade, bottle of wine, a camera and enjoy. We did see above…

Introduction

In the pages that follow we will go on a pictorial and descriptive journey through the history and splendour of the Cornish fishing village of Mousehole. I will be sharing with you our experiences of holidaying in this little piece of holiday heaven. The tiny village of Mousehole cascades down the steep hillside to its harbour where people have been watching the boats come in and out of the enclosed harbour for centuries. We truly believe that Mousehole is the jewel in the crown of Cornwall…

Introduction

If you stand at the harbour entrance in Mousehole and look out to sea you will see St Clement's Isle. This is a small rocky islet once the home of an ancient hermit that lies just offshore of the harbour wall. A few hundred yards along the coast from the village lies a huge cave which, so some people say, gives rise to the name of the village (Mouse Hole!). Car parking in the village is extremely limited with very narrow roads. Visitors to Mousehole are advised to park on the outskirts of the village and walk in. We went in late November so we were lucky enough to be able to park in the harbour front car park that overlooks the sea. Even better it was also free parking as we were staying in the winter months…

Introduction

Mousehole is an ancient fishing village in the county of Cornwall, close to the market town of Penzance. The village is home to about 830 people. It has narrow cobbled lanes where Smugglers once roamed, now peppered with art galleries, the ship inn pub, several good restaurants and small fisherman's cottages that will enchant any visitor. The horse shoe harbour where brightly coloured boats and the fishing fleet hulls reflect on the water is a charming place to dwell and pass some relaxing time in. The two sandy beaches of the harbour will beckon any sun seeker, or the close by larger pebbled beach with rock pools, where marine wonders lurk, will intrigue any small explorers, young or old armed with a net…

Introduction

The village of Mousehole, like all coastal places, has it's fair share of sea birds and wildlife. Above are just some that we encountered and enjoyed during or stay…

Introduction

Take a walk along the cliff paths that lead away from both ends of Mousehole harbour and the views all around you will steal your breath away. If you venture along the path leading from the Penzance end of the harbour you will get a view of St Clement's Isle that was once home to a hermit, or there is always the magic of St Michael's Mount also nearby that you can explore by either walking on the causeway and follow in the footsteps of ancient pilgrims, or choose to arrive by boat. Once there you will encounter the medieval masterpiece of the Castle, or the church of St Michael and All Angel's where pilgrims have been visiting since the Middle Ages. If you venture a bit further afield you can get a glimpse into the past by going to Pendeen Mining Museum that has models, and a jewellery workshop, or there is always the fabulous Geevor Tin Mine where an underground tour of this once working mine won't fail to impress the visitor. Now that we have taken the first few tentative steps to explore the area, we will, in the next chapter, learn something of the history of the village of Mousehole…

The History of Mousehole

Sitting in the sun at Mousehole

John Marius Wilson's, in 1870-72 AD, in the Imperial Gazetteer of England and Wales described Mousehole like this: **MOUSEHOLE**, a village in St. Paul parish, Cornwall; on Mounts bay, 2.25 miles South of Penzance. It was formerly called Porth-Enys; was once a market-town; was burned in 1595 by the Spaniards; is now a seat of the pilchard fishery; and has a post-office under Penzance, a coast-guard station, and a Wesleyan chapel. St. Clement's Island lies opposite the village near the shore; and had formerly a chapel. A charming terrace-road, with very fine views, goes along the margin of the bay from Mouse-hole to Penzance. Now that we know something of the origins of the village of Mousehole we will continue our historical journey of discovery…

The History of Mousehole

High and dry with fishing boat sailing by

Another famous person in **Dylan Thomas (1930 AD)** described Mousehole as ' the loveliest village in England', a title that remains true to the present day. Over the years Mousehole developed around its harbour (and of course the fishing fleet that sustained it) appearing in the record books as an important fishing port from as early as 1266 AD, in fact, part of the south quay originates from 1390 AD. Possibly the oldest pier in Cornwall. The fishing industry has declined drastically over the last 100 years, but a few fishing boats maintain the long heritage and tradition of a working harbour, whilst the majority of vessels now lying at anchor are pleasure craft…

The History of Mousehole

Boats in Mousehole harbour at low tide

One of the famous characters of Mousehole was **Dolly Pentreath**, or **Dorothy Pentreath** (baptised 1692 AD, died December 1777 AD). She was reputedly the last fluent native speaker of the Cornish language. Many accounts claim that she was the last person who spoke **only** Cornish, whilst others maintain that she could not speak a word of English until the age of twenty. Whether or not this is true, Cornish was her first language. As you walk towards the harbour from the car park, you will pass the house where she lived and it is marked by a plaque. A memorial to her is to be found in the churchyard in nearby Paul. A small village just above Mousehole…

The History of Mousehole

Looking for their tea

Mousehole's ancient name was Porth-Enys, the "port of the island", a reference to St Clement's Isle, the low rocky reef that lies just offshore and where a hermit is said to have once tended a guiding light. Opinions differ about the derivation of Mousehole's intriguing present name. One local explanation is that it may derive from the Cornish Moeshayle, meaning "at the mouth of the river of young women", but some authorities argue for the literal "mouse hole", as being a reference to the original tiny harbour, or to a nearby sea cave. There are recordings of the name Mousehole being used as far back as 1242 AD and that the names of Mousehole and Porth-Enys were used equally for many years…

The History of Mousehole

It is interesting that back in the 13th century, Mousehole was the main port in Mounts Bay and remained so well into the 16th century until Penzance and Newlyn began to gain ascendancy. In 1337 AD when Edward Woodstock, son of Edward III, became Duke of Cornwall, annual payments were levied on all ports and had to be paid to the Duchy. These were based on the number of boats fishing. In that year St. Ives was assessed at 120 shillings, Mousehole 100 shillings, Penzance 12 shillings and Newlyn 10 shillings. This means that Mousehole had the second largest fishing fleet in the area and was therefore, an important village…

The History of Mousehole

The harbour and storm waves hitting the harbour wall

Mousehole exported cured fish oil and woolen cloth to the English garrisons of Gascony in the fourteenth century and brought back, in exchange, salt for the fish curing process. Mousehole's breakwater was the earliest in Cornwall, begun in 1393 AD and so it seemed that all went well for Mousehole until the Spanish Raid of 1595 AD, after that things would never quite be the same again…

The History of Mousehole

Alan and boats on the beach at low tide

By the early 1590's, the war between Spain and England had settled into an uneasy stalemate. However, this culminated in a raid by the Spanish on Mount's Bay in July 1595 AD which had disastrous consequences for Mousehole. Control of local defence efforts in Cornwall lay in the hands of the Deputy Lieutenants, Sir William Mohun and Sir Francis Godolphin. In 1588 AD, at any rate in theory, Cornwall had claimed to be able to furnish for its defence 5,560 men, including 1,395 shot, 633 corselets, 1956 bills and halberds, 1528 bows, 4 lances and 96 light horse, and the totals were probably roughly similar seven years later…

The History of Mousehole

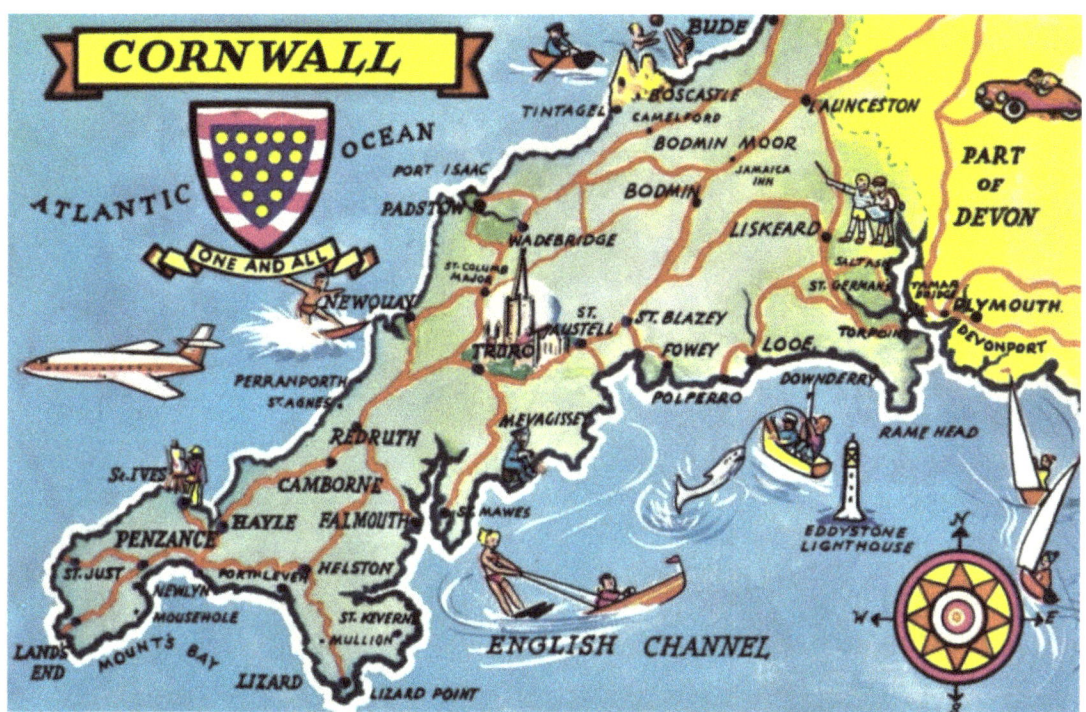

The main problem with defending Cornwall lay in its isolation, and the great length of its coastline, with its many bays and deep-water inlets which were potential landing points. Mount's Bay was singled out by the Spanish and in July 1595 AD Spanish galleys dropped anchor off Mousehole harbour to ferry ashore a force estimated at 200 pike and shot. The Spanish burnt the village and some surrounding hamlets, including the village of Paul. The inhabitants had made off in panic. However, Jenkyn Keigwin alone stood defiantly outside his home "The Keigwin" until he was shot dead by a Spaniard, the musket ball sinking deeply into the door behind him…

The History of Mousehole

The Spanish invasion gives Mousehole a special place in the history of Great Britain for whilst these invaders were soon dispatched, this event marked the last time England was ever invaded by hostile forces. Keigwin House still stands today and is the oldest house in the village, built in the 14th Century…

The History of Mousehole

It is interesting to note that even in the last century there were still hundreds of people employed in Mousehole in fishing, packing and transporting the fish. Over the years the harbour walls were gradually extended and built to cater for the hive of activity taking place. In the early 20th century, there were still over 70 commercial fishing boats based in Mousehole, mainly fishing for pilchard. It was claimed that, when the fleet was in port, you could walk across from one pier to the other without getting your feet wet by stepping across the boats moored up…

The History of Mousehole

Mousehole harbour has always been exposed to hard southerly gales. The most famous local wreck is the Thames barge, "Baltic", which was bound for Newlyn with cement when she ran onto Mousehole Island on a rough November night in 1907 AD. Her crew, and the captain's wife and daughter, were rescued by six Mousehole fishermen who manned the crabbing boat "White Lady", which had to be manhandled over the great baulks that closed the harbour mouth against the winter seas (something that continues to be done to this very day as we witnessed when we stayed there in November one year). The "Baltic" was salvaged and now lies as a hulk in a muddy creek in Essex, but a young Irish sailor onboard settled in Mousehole and married the harbour-master's daughter…

The History of Mousehole

Mousehole has proudly supplied the crews of the RNLI lifeboats even after the station was transferred in 1913 AD to the lifeboat house which still stands on Penlee. The Penlee lifeboats have carried out many heroic rescues, including saving those onboard the famous old battleship "Warspite" which, on tow for the scrap-yard, was driven ashore by a South Westerly gale at Prussia Cove on 25 April 1947 AD…

The History of Mousehole

As we have seen the village of Mousehole is not without a long and at times traumatic history. The Penlee lifeboat disaster occurred on 19 December 1981 AD off the coast of Cornwall. The Penlee Lifeboat went to the aid of the coaster Union Star after its engines failed in heavy seas. Conditions were atrocious with hurricane force winds and waves up to 60 feet high. After the lifeboat had managed to rescue four people, both vessels were lost with all hands. In all, sixteen people died including eight volunteer lifeboat-men, all from the village of Mousehole…

The History of Mousehole

The memory of the event lives on. Every year, on the 19th December, the famous Mousehole Harbour Christmas lights are switched off, in memory of those who gave their lives. This tragedy is commemorated in a Garden of Remembrance just to the north of Mousehole on the road to Newlyn at the Penlee station which was closed after the lifeboat "Solomon Browne" was lost. The present Penlee lifeboat is based in Newlyn…

The History of Mousehole

As previously mentioned during the winter months, sturdy wooden beams are used to close the harbour entrance, keeping the force of the sea at bay and protecting the village from its stormy tempest. In the past, villagers have suffered greatly from the effects of winter storms. One of these events is commemorated annually shortly before Christmas on "**Tom Bawcock's Eve**" where a monstrous fish pie is baked and consumed by the patrons of the Ship Inn on the quay side. The pie is called Star Gazy pie because it features the heads of fish staring out of the crust of he pie. This event, which becomes a major village party, attracts visitors from both the surrounding district and from all over the world…

The History of Mousehole

Despite the disaster and the relocation of the lifeboat station to Newlyn, volunteers from Mousehole have still come forward to man the boat for the R.N.L.I. The effects of the sea upon the town are also highlighted in the story of the actions of the legendary Tom Bawcock. The story goes that the people of Mousehole were suffering badly because of the huge gales and stormy seas. The fishing boats were therefore, unable to put out to sea and this resulted in the population being close to starvation. One man, by the name Tom Bawcock and his cat, braved the storm and brought back a haul of seven types of fish. The villagers were saved. By way of remembrance the village celebrate Tom's legendary deed on the 23rd of December each year when people gather to eat 'Star Gazy Pie,' so called because of the fish heads that poke out of the crust of the specially made fish pie. After enjoying this gastronomic feast we will now, in the next chapter, go **Out and About in Mousehole**…

Out and About in Mousehole

Mousehole is a magnet for visitors throughout the summer, mainly due to its picturesque beauty. The narrow streets, granite houses and stunning harbour that draws visitors by the car load every day of the year. In the winter months, when we went, it is much quieter, except that is when crowds arrive to see the harbour Christmas lights being switched on just like us. The lights switching on ceremony can attract several thousand people and range from just simple coloured lights strung between lamp posts, to the more adventurous sea serpents and sailboats fixed to the harbour wall. They are stunning!…

Out and About in Mousehole

Mousehole Christmas lights display has many aspects but one of the most interesting displays is the Celtic Cross which is located on St Clement's Island which is powered by a wind generator. The lights are switched on at 5 pm and remain on until 11 pm each night from 17th December to the 3rd January. There is, however, one exception to this continuous evening display of colour. On 19th December each year the bright lights are dimmed from 8 pm to 9 pm in memory of the brave men of the Solomon Browne Lifeboat who lost their lives on that stormy night in 1981…

Out and About in Mousehole

Star Gazy Pie in Mousehole

The Mousehole Christmas lights has, as well as familiar Christmas themes, have lights that are based on old Mousehole stories and legends. On the harbour wall below the Ship Inn you will see a Stargazey pie. Legend has it that this local fish dish was originally prepared in honour of Mousehole fisherman Tom Bawcock, who braved persistent storms to land seven different types of fish, much to the relief of Mousehole residents who'd gone without food for a fortnight. Every year on 23rd December it is remembered on Tom Bawcock's Eve, Stargazey pie is cooked and served at the Ship Inn. Another story you may hear is that of the Mousehole Cat, the subject of the well-known children's book by Antonia Barber…

Out and About in Mousehole

As I have already mentioned the Mousehole Christmas light display usually starts around the middle of December and continues to the end of the first week in January. The lights are switched on at around five pm and are turned off at eleven pm. On the 19th December the lights are dimmed between eight and nine pm in memory of the crew of the Penlee lifeboat Solomon Browne which was lost with its entire crew of eight on 19 December 1981 while attempting to rescue the crew of the MV Union Star in hurricane force winds. The eight crew aboard the Union Star also died. 2019, will see the 56th display of Christmas lights in Mousehole harbour. The lights are created, maintained and erected by volunteers from Mousehole itself and are funded by contributions from the public. Susie and I watched them putting the lights up and testing them while we were recently there on holiday in November…

Out and About in Mousehole

"The Mousehole Cat" is a children's book written by Antonia Barber and illustrated by Nicola Bayley. It is based on the legend of Cornish fisherman Tom Bawcock and the Stargazey pie. It tells the tale of a cat who goes with its owner on a fishing expedition in rough seas. The book has won awards for Illustrated Children's Book of the Year. It has since been adapted into a 1994 animated film, a puppet show and is also being adapted as a stage musical…

Out and About in Mousehole

The story of the Mousehole Cat tell of one very stormy winter, when none of the fishermen of the village of Mousehole had been able to leave the harbour for a long while and the village is near starvation. Tom Bawcock and his loyal black and white cat called Mowzer, decide to brave the storms and set sail to catch some fish. When the boat hits the storm, it is represented by a giant "Storm-Cat", which allows Mowzer to eventually save the day by soothing the storm with her purring. This purring becomes a song and while the Storm-Cat is resting Tom is able to haul in his catch and return to harbour. When they arrive back at the village, the entire catch is cooked into various dishes, including fifty Stargazey pies, on which all of the villagers then feasted themselves on!…

Out and About in Mousehole

Boats at anchor in Mousehole harbour

Mousehole has a horse shoe harbour where brightly coloured pleasure boats and the fishing fleet bob up and down and reflect in the water. It is a very charming place to dwell and just relax. The two sandy beaches in the harbour will beckon you to enjoy the sunset, or you can view it from the larger pebbled beach with it's rock pools where marine wonders lurk. A walk along the cliff paths leading from Mousehole harbour is where the views of the ocean will steal your breath away. You can also see St Clement's Isle that was once home to a hermit and in the distance is the magic of St Michael's Mount highlighted in the evening sunset. Life can not get much better than this, so as the sunsets, we will reluctantly leave the village of Mousehole and venture further afield and visit some of the beautiful Gardens of Cornwall…

The Gardens of Cornwall

Bosvigo Gardens

Bosvigo gardens has 3 acres of intimate gardens surrounding the charming, mainly Georgian house (not open to the public). The owners, have developed a series of enchanting enclosed gardens or out-door rooms each with their own colour theme. Unlike many Cornish gardens Bosvigo does not rely on spring-flowering shrubs for its colour but on summer-flowering herbaceous plants. In the summer months a dazzling display of yellows, reds and other hot colours contrast with the unusual black and green garden to the rear of the house. The pink and grey garden is especially pretty. Bosvigo specialises in hellebores and there are also some interesting pulmonarias. The plants man will find much of interest in this immaculately kept garden. The nursery also has interesting perennial and herbaceous plants available for sale…

The Gardens of Cornwall

Glendurgan Gardens

Glendurgan gardens is a delightful garden set above the Helford River in one of the three valleys which converge at Durgan. In 1820 the valley was purchased by Alfred Fox, who set about creating an informal garden. His family had established a thriving shipping company in nearby Falmouth during the 18th century. The Fal estuary, a great deep water harbour, was once the first port of call for shipping returning from Africa, the Americas, the Far East and the Antipodes. The family shipping company provided a perfect vehicle for importing plants from all over the world. Alfred Fox built the unpretentious, creeper-clad house (not open to the public) at the top of the valley soon after coming to Glendurgan…

The Gardens of Cornwall

Glendurgan Gardens

The house looks out over an expanse of grass towards Helford, the view framed by foliage. Many of the fine old trees were planted by Alfred Fox including the two splendid tulip trees below the house. He was also responsible for the many serpentine paths laid out in the romantic taste. In 1833 he planted the laurel maze. The gently curving silvery-grey hedges of the maze, set out on a slope, resemble a serpent curled up on the grass. This unusual and popular feature has recently been restored. Alfred Fox passed on his interests and talents to his successors and three subsequent generations of the family carried on the gardening tradition. They enhanced and enriched the garden, introducing some of the species that contribute to the gardens great character…

The Gardens of Cornwall

Headland Gardens

Headland gardens is a splendid cliff garden and is bounded by the sea on three sides. The 1.5 acre site is 100 feet above sea level and, although the views are spectacular, the owners have to contend with gales and salt spray, which can blow in from any of the three sides. To overcome these difficulties the owners have used narrow paths, hedges and archways to create hidden areas. Here sub-tropical plants thrive in the shelter provided. The owners are particularly fond of Australian and New Zealand species. The garden, which has some rare plants, is always full of interest. A flight of 100 steps leads down to a cove and from here visitors may swim in the sea if they wish…

The Gardens of Cornwall

The Lost Gardens of Heligan

The award-winning Lost Gardens of Heligan are made up of 200 acres of working productive gardens and pleasure grounds. Twenty-five years ago, Heligan's historic gardens were unknown and unseen; lost under a tangle of weeds. It was only the chance discovery of a door in the ruins that led to the restoration of this once great estate. Today, the Lost Gardens of Heligan have been put back where they belong: in pride of place amongst the finest gardens in Cornwall…

The Gardens of Cornwall

The Lost Gardens of Heligan

There have been gardens at Heligan since 1603. The gardens were formalized and expanded in the early 18th century and reached their present size in 1780. The Heligan estate, in the hands of the Tremayne family, had its heyday during the reign of Queen Victoria. In the 20th century the gardens fell into a decline and were virtually abandoned between the years 1914 to 1991. Since that time the gardens have become the largest garden restoration project in Europe. Huge quantities of fallen timber and brambles have been removed revealing 2.5 miles of footpaths hidden for 50 years. The footpaths wander between the alpine Ravine, the walled gardens and glass-houses, the vinery, the Melon Yard, the Crystal Grotto, the Summer-houses, the Italian Garden, the 22 acre sub-tropical Jungle valley brimming with exotic foliage and many other wonderful features…

The Gardens of Cornwall

The Lost Gardens of Heligan

The gardens at Heligan has woodland and farm walks through beautiful and sustain-ably-managed Cornish countryside, and a pioneering conservation project offers visitors a close-up view of the wildlife resident on the estate. Over 5,000 new trees have been planted to provide shelter and care has been taken to conform to the original planting in all parts of the gardens. The Heligan project is still ongoing with the gardens now an example of a living and working museum of 19th century horticulture…

The Gardens of Cornwall

Penjerrick Gardens

This peaceful 15 acre spring-flowering garden with fine views of the sea has considerable historical and botanical interest. Penjerrick was created 200 years ago by the Fox family (who were also responsible for the gardens at Glendurgan). The family planted the upper garden with specimens collected abroad including rhododendrons, camellias, magnolias, azaleas, tree ferns and bamboos. The garden is also the home of the Penjerrick and Barclayi hybrid rhododendrons. The lower part of Penjerrick is a luxuriant valley garden reached by a wooden bridge. In this wild, jungle-like setting are ponds, bluebells and tree ferns that date back almost to the original planting of the garden. The tranquil garden is at its very best in the spring…

The Gardens of Cornwall

Trebah Gardens

Trebah garden is a spectacular 25 acre ravine garden that falls 200 feet to a private beach on the River Helford. The sub-tropical garden is now 150 years old and leads from an 18th century house down a steep, wooded valley to a sheltered cove. The lawns at the top of the garden provide a splendid view over the sub-tropical jungle where vast Australian tree-ferns and palms tower over 100 year old rhododendrons, magnolias and camellias. Banana and bamboo trees are among a huge collection of rare sub-tropical trees and shrubs. A stream cascades down the garden over waterfalls, through ponds with exotic water plants and Koi Carp and winds through 2 acres of white and blue hydrangeas to finally rush out over the beach. The cove has a memorial to those men who left the tiny jetty to take part in the Dunkirk landings but did not sadly return…

The Gardens of Cornwall

Trelissick Gardens

The Trelissick estate stands at the head of the estuary of the River Fal. Here a great stretch of deep water runs far inland with smaller creeks and inlets branching off on either side. Wooded slopes lead down to the water with oaks and beeches overhanging the mud-flats of the tidal creeks. The King Harry Ferry below Trelissick is the only connection across the water to the Roseland peninsular on the other side of the estuary. In about 1750 a modest villa was built at Trelissick on the foundations of an earlier building. This house was re-modelled in 1825 by Peter Frederick Robinson who added the columned portico which rises to the height of the south front. Robinson's patron was Thomas Daniell whose father had bought the estate in 1800 with the fortune he inherited from tin-mining interests…

The Gardens of Cornwall

Trelissick Gardens

Thomas Daniell planted much of the woodland along the shores of the estuary and the carriage drives he laid out in the park are now shady woodland walks. Between 1844 and 1913 the estate was owned by the Gilbert family who made great improvements to the grounds. They planted ornamental woodlands and some of the huge holm oaks and conifers in the garden. The wonderful garden seen today was largely created by the present owners who inherited Trelissick in 1937. From the house (not open to the public) and the drive there are splendid views across a great sweep of grass to the Carrick Roads. On clear days Pendennis Castle can be seen on a promontory in the far distance…

The Gardens of Cornwall

Trengwainton Gardens

This 98 acre shrub garden, overlooking Mount's Bay, climbs gently uphill for a third of a mile following a little stream. Trengwainton faces due south and has a wonderfully mild climate, rarely experiencing hard frosts. As a result tender and half-hardy trees, shrubs and other plants have been established here that cannot be grown in the open anywhere else in England. Trengwainton is largely a 20th century creation although there has been a house here at least since the 16th century. Lieutenant Colonel Sir Edward Bolitho, whose family came here in 1857, began work on the garden after he inherited the rambling Victorian house in 1925…

The Gardens of Cornwall

Trengwainton Gardens

The framework of the garden dates back to the early 19th century when Rose Price, the son of a wealthy West Indian sugar planter, planted the tall beeches and oaks that line the stream and shelter the house. Without these trees Trengwainton would suffer the full force of the westerly gales. Price also used much of his income from the Jamaican plantations to create the unusual walled garden at the foot of the drive. He used brick, a warmer but more expensive material than the local granite, to build a series of compartments. The dividing walls between each separate garden have a steeply sloped bed of banked-up soil on their western side. This is a rare survival of a practice that was common in the late 18th and early 19th centuries and the south- and west-facing slopes receive the full benefit of the sun. Here early crops of vegetables are produced and tender plants are cultivated…

The Gardens of Cornwall

Trevarno Gardens

This un-spoilt Cornish estate is a tranquil haven that has been protected for 700 years. The beautiful Georgian and Victorian gardens at Trevarno contain an extensive collection of rare trees and shrubs. There are also numerous garden features and follies. Other highlights include walled gardens and woodland walks, where abundant wildlife can be seen. It is also possible to follow the progress of Trevarno's major restoration and conservation projects. The Garden Museum at Trevarno contains an intriguing collection of tools and implements. The splendid Fountain Garden Conservatory allows visitors to admire the plants and enjoy some refreshments whatever the weather. Having visited many of the lovely gardens of Cornwall it is now time for us to invade (visit) the majestic Castles of Cornwall…

The Castles of Cornwall

St Mawes Castle

In the late 1530's Henry VIII was under threat of war from France and Spain because he had divorced his Catholic wife, Catherine of Aragon. He immediately set about the fortification of the south coast. Between 1540 and 1545 the River Fal was given two forts to protect it, St Mawes on the east bank and Pendennis on the west. St Mawes castle stands on the low Roseland Peninsula and its main building consisted of a central tower entirely surrounded by three lobes shaped like a clover leaf. Pendennis castle was a simple round tower and gate enclosed by a lower curtain wall…

The Castles of Cornwall

St Mawes Pendennis Castle

In Elizabethan times an encircling wall and bastions were built at Pendennis. The second St Mawes castle, to be built, had more care spent on it with good quality stone and decorative carvings. In 1595 the Spanish attacked Penzance and the River Fal's garrisons were hurriedly reinforced. However the Spanish invasion never came and the only attack on the castles came during the Civil War. Pendennis being on high ground, dominating its peninsula, held out for six months in 1646 against the Parliamentarians. Apart from Raglan Castle it was the last to surrender to Cromwell's forces. St Mawes, in contrast was in a weak position half way up a hill with no defences from a landward attack. The governor immediately surrendered. In more recent times the two forts were used as barracks and in both World Wars were included in Britain's coastal defence…

The Castles of Cornwall

Tintagel Castle

In 1139 Geoffrey de Monmouth published his 'History of Britain' and claimed that Tintagel was the birthplace of King Arthur. Although there may have been the remains of the community established by St Juliot in the 6th century, when Reginald, Earl of Cornwall built his stronghold here in 1145 there was no record of Arthur's castle. Reginald, the illegitimate son of Henry I, was responsible for the Great Hall and Chapel. In the middle of the 13th century further buildings were added by Earl Richard, the younger brother of Henry III…

The Castles of Cornwall

Tintagel Castle

In the 14th century, with other Cornish castles, it was passed into the ownership of the Black Prince. He carried out some restoration but after his death the castle fell into decline. It was used as a prison at the end of the 14th century but was never used again as a fortress. Today it forms part of the Duchy of Cornwall. Coastal erosion has resulted in the castle being partly on the mainland and partly on a peninsula. There is a narrow causeway today that connects the castle to the mainland guarded by the statue of the great King Arthur…

The Castles of Cornwall

Caerhays Castle

Although Caerhays Castle has the appearance of a Norman stronghold it was in fact built in the 19th century for John Bettesworth Trevanion. The estate that he inherited in 1801, at the age of 21, had been in the hands of the Trevanion family since 1390. The fashionable architect, John Nash, was employed to create the splendid mansion. However, Nash proved very expensive and this, together with the cost of building such an impressive home, ruined the family. In 1840 the family were heavily in debt and fled to Paris, where John Trevanion died…

The Castles of Cornwall

Caerhays Castle

The castle fell into disrepair until 13 years later it was bought by Michael Williams, a Cornish Member of Parliament. He was also a prominent mine owner and industrialist and, together with his son John, set about the restoration of the castle. Later generations of the Williams family created the 60 acres of informal woodlands and gardens that surround the house. At the turn of the century J C Williams arranged plant gathering trips to China. The gardens are famous for their magnolias, camellias, oaks and rhododendrons. The fifth generation of the Williams family still lives at the castle. Today Caerhays is one of the few remaining Nash built castles. In the next chapter, having wandered around some of the Cornish gardens and visited the castles of Cornwall we will venture inside the historical houses owned by the people of Cornwall…

The Historical Houses of Cornwall

Antony House

Antony House was built between 1711 and 1721 for Sir William Carew, whose family have owned the estate since 1492. The house stands on an isolated peninsular bounded by the estuaries of the Rivers Tamar and Lyner to the east and north and by the sea to the south. The building consists of a central block faced with silver-grey stone and two brick wings joined by colonnades. Apart from the addition of a 19th century porch the house has not been altered since. Unlike many country houses Antony was spared the modernisation of the Victorian period. Antony House is exceptional for the quality of its furnishings. The rooms are panelled in Dutch oak and some contain the original 18th century furniture. They also display some fine china, tapestries, embroideries and many interesting portraits. Antony House has paintings and treasures belonging to the generations of the Carew family who lived at the estate before this house was built and those who have lived there since. The splendid collection of portraits includes work by Reynolds and a painting of Charles I at his trial. A portrait of Richard Carew, the historian and author of the 'Survey of Cornwall' who inherited the estate in 1564 faces Charles across the entrance hall…

The Historical Houses of Cornwall

Godolphin House

Is a granite-built Tudor and Stuart house. The house seen today is a remnant of a far larger building that was the home of the Godolphin family until the middle of the 18th century. The Godolphin's, who made their wealth from the local tin-mining industry, were one of the leading families of west Cornwall. By the mid-16th century the house consisted of three ranges of buildings with the courtyard closed off by a crenellated wall on the north side. Sir William Godolphin, a soldier in the service of Henry VIII, made some alterations to the house and further work was carried out at the end of the 16th century by Sir Francis Godolphin, Governor of the Scilly Isles…

The Historical Houses of Cornwall

Godolphin House

The present north or entrance range of the house was probably added in the 1630's to replace a screen wall. In the mid-17th century the building reached its heyday and by 1689 Godolphin House contained around 100 rooms. William Godolphin's grandson, Sidney, was Queen Ann's Lord Treasurer between 1702 and 1710 and was responsible for financing the Duke of Marlborough's wars. He was created Earl of Godolphin and his son married Marlborough's daughter. The 1st Earl spent little time at Godolphin House and the 2nd Earl even less. On the death of the 2nd Earl in 1766 the estate passed through his daughter to the Duke of Leeds. In 1805 a considerable part of the building was pulled down, including the 16th century hall, and Godolphin became simply a Cornish farmhouse…

The Historical Houses of Cornwall

Lanhydrock House

The Lanhydrock estate was bought in 1620 by Sir Richard Robartes, a Truro banker. In 1624 he was created a baron by James I and in 1630 he set about building the magnificent Tudor mansion. However, he did not live to see the completion of his work and the house was finished by his son in 1651. In 1881 a disastrous fire destroyed nearly all the building. Only the north wing, the entrance porch and gatehouse remain from the original house. However, the owner, Lord Robartes, had the house rebuilt as a replica of what had been burned. The same grey granite was used and the result is a pleasing symmetrical composition ranged round three sides of a courtyard. The tour of the house includes 49 rooms and reflects all aspects of Victorian life above and below stairs. The kitchen, larders and dairy still contain the utensils and equipment needed to fed the great household and the cellars, bake-house and servants' quarters are also on show. In the family's apartments the Long Gallery in the original wing is most impressive. It has a superb plaster ceiling depicting scenes from the Old Testament and was created in the mid-17th century by local craftsmen…

The Historical Houses of Cornwall

Mount Edgcumbe House

The Tudor home of the Earls of Mount Edgcumbe, has a dramatic view over Plymouth Sound, one of England's finest natural harbours. In the early-16th century the estate which includes the Rame peninsular came by marriage to Sir Piers Edgcumbe. His family seat was ten miles to the north at Cotehele. In 1539 Sir Piers created a deer park at Mount Edgcumbe and in 1547 his son Richard engaged Roger Palmer, a local mason, to build a new house high on the hillside overlooking the harbour. The house was built to a compact rectangular plan with a top-lit hall in the centre and circular corner towers. When the Edgcumbes abandoned Cotehele in the late 17th century Mount Edgcumbe became their main family seat. During the 18th and early-19th century the family carried out much internal re-modelling of the house and some external rebuilding…

The Historical Houses of Cornwall

Mount Edgcumbe House

In 1749 the corner towers were altered into their present octagonal form by Richard, 1st Lord Edgcumbe. Lord Edgcumbe's son, an admiral, became 1st Earl of Mount Edgcumbe in 1789. The 1st Earl and his son transformed the grounds at Mount Edgcumbe into one of the finest landscape gardens in England. Today the Grade I listed gardens, Cornwall's earliest landscaped park, are mostly unchanged but in 1941 the house was gutted by German bombers during their Blitz on Plymouth. The building was left as a ruin until 1958 when the 6th Earl commissioned Adrian Gilbert Scott to rebuild it using a steel frame and concrete floors. In 1971 the house and 865 acres of grounds were bought by Plymouth City Council and Cornwall County Council. The grounds were then turned into a country park…

The Historical Houses of Cornwall

St Michael's Mount

The great granite crag of St Michael's Mount is dedicated to the archangel St Michael who, according to legend, appeared here in 495. Edward the Confessor founded a chapel on the Mount in 1044 in a grant to the Benedictine Abbey of Mont Saint Michael in Brittany. In 12th century when Richard I was on Crusade a group of John's supporters seized the Mount to hold as a fortress. Later it reverted to monastic use but was treated again as a stronghold in the Wars of the Roses and the Cornish Rebellion against Edward VI. During the Civil War the Mount was held for the King but surrendered to the Parliamentarians in 1646. In 1660 the Mount was bought by Sir John St Aubyn and since that time it has had a peaceful existence…

The Historical Houses of Cornwall

St Michael's Mount

The Mount remained mostly unoccupied, except for occasional use during the summer months, until the late 18th century when the family began to set up a more permanent residence. Despite the difficulties of building on a great rock cut off at every high tide the family constructed a great new wing. The impressive Victorian apartments are decorated with fine plaster relief's and contain some Chippendale furniture. The Mount remained in the ownership of the St Aubyn family until 1964 when it was given to the National Trust by the 3rd Lord St Levan. St Michael's Mount is an island at high tide and a romantic sight. From its terraces splendid views can be seen towards Land's End and the Lizard. The slopes have sub-tropical vegetation planted by the St Aubyn family. At the water's edge there is a small harbour-side community with shops and restaurants…

The Historical Houses of Cornwall

Trerice House

Is a small Elizabethan manor house built of buff-coloured limestone. The house is set in a quiet valley, approached by a narrow, winding lane. It was built in 1573 by Sir John Arundell on the site of an earlier house. He inherited the property from his father and with it the means to rebuild the house. His father, also Sir John, had a successful and lucrative career in the service of the Crown. He was knighted after the battle of the Spurs, was Esquire of the Body to Henry VIII and also served under Edward VI and Queen Mary. The Arundell family supported the Crown during the Civil War with some costs but recovered their position after the Restoration…

The Historical Houses of Cornwall

Trerice House

The house escaped alteration during the 18th and 19th centuries, probably because its owners chose to live elsewhere. Trerice remained in the ownership of the Arundell's for over 400 years but in 1802 it passed to the Acland family of Killerton in Devon. The property was sold in 1915 and changed hands several times before it was purchased by the National Trust in 1953. Trerice has a traditional E-shaped facade with decorative scrolled gables in the Dutch style. These are unusual in Cornwall and probably reflect Sir John Arundell's service in the Low Countries for Elizabeth I. The bay to the left of the entrance porch is completely filled by the window that lights the great hall. Many of the 576 panes are the original 16th century glass…

The Historical Houses of Cornwall

Trewithen House

Is a fine early Georgian squire's house set in a splendid woodland garden. The name Trewithen means 'house of the trees'. The house was created by three generations of the Hawkins family. Philip Hawkins, the younger son of a rich lawyer and MP, bought the estate in the early 18th century. He commissioned the architect Thomas Edwards of Greenwich to extend and remodel the five bay brick house. The work on the house continued after the death of Philip Hawkins in 1738 and in 1763 - 64 his nephew, Thomas, engaged the renowned London architect, Sir Robert Taylor, to remodel some of the interior…

The Historical Houses of Cornwall

Trewithen House

Thomas Hawkins also created the present forecourt and landscaped the grounds. He died after being inoculated for smallpox in 1766. The estate passed to his son Christopher, who carried out some minor internal alterations in the late-18th and early-19th centuries but since then there have been few structural changes to the house. In 1904 Trewithen was inherited by George Johnstone after the male line of the Hawkins family had died out. The present owner is his grandson. The original five-bay house purchased by Philip Hawkins was extended by two bays on either side and the north side (now the entrance front) was covered with plaster. The south facade, constructed from local grey Pentewan stone, was probably begun in 1738, the year Philip Hawkins died. This dignified facade looks out over a lawn encircled by trees planted by George Johnstone. As we leave the great houses of Cornwall we will, in the next chapter, swoop down into many of the beautiful Towns and Villages of Cornwall…

The Towns and Villages of Cornwall

Bodmin

Is on the edge of the famous Bodmin Moor. Bodmin was once a place of pilgrimage with a shrine to St Petroc who travelled from Padstow to Bodmin to form a monastery, now long gone following the Reformation. The 15th century parish church, the largest in Cornwall, still bears his name. The town was once the most important stannary, a tin market, based on tin workings in the area. In the 15th and 16th centuries Bodmin was the base for several Cornish rebellions against the state, but none of these were successful and the leaders were hanged. Today this small market town is very much a regional centre for this part of Cornwall, and makes a good touring base for exploring further afield. If you walk around the town you will see that many of the historic buildings have been restored, including the impressive Shire Hall, once used as a courtroom…

The Towns and Villages of Cornwall

Bolventor

Bolventor is a small hamlet on the main road, but you get the best views of Bodmin moor from here, including Brown Willy and Rough Tor, the main tors. Bolventor is famous for its pub, Jamaica Inn, as it featured in the book by Daphne du Maurier. This is somewhat a bleak area but surprisingly quite a lot to see and visit nearby. See if you can catch sight of the '*Beast of Bodmin*', an allegedly loose big cat, although this is similar to the one also spotted on Exmoor! If you want to walk up Rough Tor, go on the A39 and turn south just west of Camelford, it is signposted and there is a car-park…

The Towns and Villages of Cornwall

Boscastle

Boscastle is in a dramatic location with the small village in the folds of high steep cliffs where two rivers, the Valency and the Jordon meet. If you start walking at the back of the National Trust car park, the path takes you along the river banks. Boscastle's harbour, with its stone hollow jetty, leads you to a long street that meanders up to woodland. The small port was used, in the past, for loading slate from the quarries, the ships being pulled in by small boats and horses. A blowhole in the cliff face, *Devils Bellows*, shows you the power of the water…

The Towns and Villages of Cornwall

Boscastle

Boscastle is a Cornish coastal location that is dramatic in winter, and very busy in summer with tourists. Boscastle's famous connections include Turner painting the harbour and Thomas Hardy marrying the vicar's daughter. More recently the village became even more well-known when it suffered considerable structural damage in a flash flood in August 2004, with helicopters rescuing stranded residents. Today the village buildings have been restored and new flood prevention measures introduced. This is a lovely place to visit, but take great care when walking on the cliff paths…

The Towns and Villages of Cornwall

Bude

Bude is a North Cornwall seaside resort with a small but busy town centre. A very popular holiday resort in summer as it has good beaches, especially Sumerleaze Beach, and can be combined with walks over the cliff tops on the South West Coast Path and days out along the coast. Both the two extensive beaches, Sumerleaze and Crooklets, are ideal for families and the breakwaters give the younger ones a chance to try crabbing or to spot the local wildlife and other seaside creatures…

The Towns and Villages of Cornwall

Bude

In Bude a small canal in the town runs down to the sea and is used for boating, and this canal reflects Bude's past as a busy port. The town centre has a range of shops and there is wide choice of accommodation to fit nearly every budget. For a night out there are plenty of night clubs together with entertainment in the pubs. Bude runs a popular Jazz festival every year. On the outskirts of the town is a large, modern swimming pool…

The Towns and Villages of Cornwall

Callington

Callington is a small town on the Tavistock to Liskeard road. There are lots of walks around the area and the town makes a good centre for touring this part of Cornwall and over the border into Devon as well as the lovely Tamar Valley. One nice walk is up Kit Hill to the Kit Hill Country Park which has an 800 foot chimney which reflects the areas important 18th century copper mining. In the town itself are small shops and an unusual mural trail to follow. Visit the Heritage Centre here to find out more about the towns history…

The Towns and Villages of Cornwall

Camborne

Camborne is famous for the Camborne School of Mines which is now part of Exeter University. The town was once the centre of the Cornish tin mining industry, but now all of the mines are closed. The last one that closed, South Crofty mine, is near the town. The steam locomotion pioneer Richard Trevithick lived here, he was born in 1771 AD. He invented the 'Puffing Devil' which was the first steam-powered road locomotive. A Trevithick Day is held every year on the last day of April and featuring steam engines. If you are visiting Camborne, pick up a 'Town Trail' leaflet and take the route to see historical buildings and places including the Old Market House, the statue of Trevithick and the Parish Church…

The Towns and Villages of Cornwall

Camelford

Camelford is a bit of a bottleneck as the main A39 road narrows here and creates delays in the summer. The traffic wardens are active to keep the road clear as the main road is also the High Street with many small local shops. Camelford is on the River Camel, and you can walk or ride a bike along the river bank, which is a popular thing to do here whilst on holiday in the summer. If you are visiting, park at the car park by the river. In the town is a small Market Place next to the main road, which has a Methodist Church that was visited by John Wesley. Camelford is also said to be the site of Camelot. It is said that King Arthur fell at Slaughter Bridge, a mile or so north of Camelford on the B3314, or so they will tell you...

The Towns and Villages of Cornwall

Cawsand

Cawsand is a small village that overlooks Plymouth Sound from the Cornish side and is tucked away with its neighbour Kingsand. You can walk to the headland, Rame Head, from here and just beyond that is the long beach of Whitesand Bay that stretches westwards towards Looe. The village, once a smuggling centre, is part of the Mount Edgcumbe Country Park, and there is an old 19th century fort, now converted into a residence. This is quite a good location for a quiet holiday with Cawsand's small beach, one pub, and a hotel. There is a summer ferry service that will take you into Plymouth for a day out. The pleasant river trip takes about an hour…

The Towns and Villages of Cornwall

Dobwalls

Dobwalls is a small village which is mainly passed through now, as the popular local miniature railway and adventure park near the village closed down in 2007. The A38 now bypasses Dobwalls. If you are staying near here Bodmin Moor is just to the north of the village…

The Towns and Villages of Cornwall

Fowey

Fowey is on the estuary of the River Fowey and is a lovely spot to visit or stay. It has a harbour and quaint narrow streets that twist through the village. Historically the village has been home to pirates and smugglers, the 18th century Cornish smuggler, John Carter, lived in Fowey. There are some shops, mainly small retailers on Fore Street, as well as places to eat and drink…

The Towns and Villages of Cornwall

Fowey

In Fowey you can take a passenger ferry to Polruan across the river to Bodinnick, and a nearby car ferry connects with Bodinnick. In the summer, running from Easter through to October, a number of boats run trips on the river. The harbour is very popular with yachtsmen, and large cargo ships still load up exports of china clay from Fowey. Local events include the annual Fowey Royal Regatta, which takes place in August, and the Fowey Festival of Music and Words every May. Fowey's most famous resident was the author Daphne du Maurier…

The Towns and Villages of Cornwall

Falmouth

Falmouth is a busy Cornish port and resort, with a large harbour. There is a local fishing fleet and boat yards, and the large dry dock handles tankers and other vessels. Smaller leisure craft use the Falmouth yachting centre. The port was a busy place in the 17th and 18th century with the mail packet service mail boats coming in. Falmouth has a famous local paper, called the *Falmouth Packet*, which brought the first news of the Battle of Trafalgar to England. Today shark fishing is popular, with day trips for visitors, and boat trips are available up the estuary of the rivers Fal and Penryn. Good beaches are to be found just a short walk from the town centre under the cliff tops, with Gyllyngvase beach being the most popular…

The Towns and Villages of Cornwall

Falmouth

While in Falmouth a walk up to Pendennis Castle on the headland gives you really great views over the coastline. Historically, the town was established by the Killigrew family, who were pirates and smugglers. A walk around the town and you will see Falmouth's historic buildings that include Pendennis Castle, the customs house, and Grove Hill House. Due to the mild climate the parks and gardens are a real delight. Gyllyngdune Gardens has a Pavilion, bandstand and a secret grotto! Car parking has always been a problem, so visitors can now park up the Penryn estuary at Ponsharden, off the A39, and take a ferry down to Custom House Quay, although there is also a bus service…

The Towns and Villages of Cornwall

Hayle

Hayle is located right on the river Hayle estuary, just inland from St Ives Bay. The town has a smallish shopping centre, but is popular because of the three miles of beaches in the area, and it makes a good base for touring the North Cornwall coastline. Despite early Bronze Age and Roman settlements the town only came into existence during the Industrial Revolution due to the copper and tin mining industry. Hayle became one of the largest ports in Cornwall by the middle of the 19th century, mainly exporting and importing by boats going across to South Wales…

The Towns and Villages of Cornwall

Hayle

In Hayle the local company called Harvey & Co exported its Cornish beam engines all over the world. Over the years the port declined along with the tin and copper industry and today the port is mainly used by pleasure craft. The local place names and street names in Hayle still reflect the tin and copper industry of the past, such as Foundry Square and Copperpool. This is a nice place for a holiday with coastal areas to explore, including the sand dunes and beaches close by. Being in an estuary Hayle is important for wildlife and the tidal flats are a popular destination for bird watchers. For water sports Gwithian beach near Godrevy is the place to go. Accommodation in Hayle ranges from holiday villages to small hotels and guest houses…

The Towns and Villages of Cornwall

Helston

Helston was formally a port until the Looe Bar formed across the River Cober forming Looe Pool. The town, like so many, grew with the Cornish tin mining industry. It's well worth walking around to see the Regency houses in the town along Cross Street, the old well, and the Victorian Guildhall. Coinagehall Street has a monument to Humphrey Millett Grylls, a local man who saved the Wheal Vor from closure, preserving the jobs of over 1000 men. The mine is now, however, closed. Locals and visitors enjoy the floral dance that happens through the streets of Helston with the Furry Dance, this event has lots of colour and music, but only on May 8th. Unless that's a Sunday or Monday, when the dance is done on the Saturday before. A great local event to witness. They say that sometime ago a dragon dropped a rock on the town, but the town survived, or so the tale goes…

The Towns and Villages of Cornwall

Kilkhampton

Kilkhampton is a small village with a few shops and pubs, but close to pretty country lanes and fine beaches. It gets busy in Kilkhampton during the summer months as it is on a main route along the North Cornish coast. Just by the public car park you will find a nice 12-15th century church, St. James standing back from the main road. Inside the church is a memorial to Sir Bevil Grenville who was a leader of the Royalists during the English Civil War, he is buried in the graveyard…

The Towns and Villages of Cornwall

Land's End

Most people know that Land's End is the southernmost end of England, right at the end of Cornwall. The site is privately owned with the nearest village being Sennen. The tourist centre at Land's End has gift shops, cafes, exhibitions, audio-visual presentations, play areas, a 4D cinema, and a farm to keep the visitor amused. Of course it has what is probably the famous signpost in the UK, erected in the 1950's showing you how far it is to some places faraway, where you can pay to have your photo taken with the signpost showing the place of your choice. Note that nearly all the attractions at Land's End have an extra charge…

The Towns and Villages of Cornwall

Land's End

At Land's End, although you have to pay for the car-park, you can walk along the cliff paths here and see some dramatic views over this part of the Cornish coast. They have a Heritage Trail here, and you can get a map of the walks at the Visitor Centre. Land's End is, of course, famous as the starting, or finishing, point for many record breaking attempts, by just about all means of transport, to and from John O'Groats in Scotland. The site is complete with a finishing/starting line, depending on which way you went, so you can record your achievement…

The Towns and Villages of Cornwall

Reiki the Cats of Cornwall

Lanreath

Lanreath is a very small Cornish village of about 500 people tucked away in the hills inland. There is a church here, St Marnarck's, which has some interesting woodcarvings. Lanreath's main 'claim to fame' is a ghost story. It is claimed that a ghost was seen, dressed all in black, driving a coach which was being pulled by a headless horse…

The Towns and Villages of Cornwall

Launceston

Launceston is an old Cornish town, set on a hill at a major road junction, with a compact shopping centre. Launceston was once the county capital until the 19th century and even had its own mint up to the 13th century. A visit to Launceston is ideal if you like churches, try St Mary Magdalene for its unique 16th century granite carving, St Thomas's for the largest font in Cornwall, and St Stephen-by-Launceston, 1.5 miles north by the Golf Club, as this church was the mother church of the town. Get a 'Town Trail' leaflet which will guide you through the streets and notable buildings, including the castle, which is also the start of the 'Two Castles Trail' to Okehampton Castle and the Tamar Valley Discovery Trail. The countryside around Launceston includes the Tamar Valley, is popular for self-catering holidays due to its central location near the Cornish border with Devon…

The Towns and Villages of Cornwall

Liskeard

Liskeard is an old Cornish market town with fine houses, and it gets very busy in the summer. Liskeard was a stannary town where tin miners brought their tin for weighing, assaying and taxation. The town's growth in the 19th century was purely due to the mining industry and the arrival of the railway. The whole town centre is largely Victorian, being designed by the architect Henry Rice. Market day (every other Tuesday) is busy in Liskeard as it is a premier cattle market for the surrounding area. The main shopping area is centred on Fore Street, which is pedestrianised, and there is a good range of shops here…

The Towns and Villages of Cornwall

Liskeard

In Liskeard you can pick up a copy of the 'Liskeard Heritage Trail' at the recently restored Stuart House when you visit as it's worth-while seeing the other historic buildings in Liskeard which include the Guildhall and the Pipe Well, the water of which is said to have healing powers. A Bull Stone can be seen in the castle park, were the 'sport' of bull-baiting once took place. Liskeard also has a Leisure Centre with an indoor swimming pool. You can also walk along part of the old Canal which went down to Looe...

The Towns and Villages of Cornwall

Looe

Looe is two small fishing villages called East and West Looe, and are joined by a bridge over the River Looe. Once a thriving port exporting copper, Looe declined during the 1800's even though a canal was built to the railway station in Liskeard to take goods down to the port. Today, Looe is a lovely place to visit and it is dependent on tourism and a small fishing fleet. West Looe has a church with separate bell tower, whilst East Looe, with a sandy beach, has small streets in a grid-like pattern. Whilst here you could try your hand at shark or mackerel fishing, day trips are available. Looe gets very busy with tourists in summer as it is so popular, so escape the crowd by going on a boat trip to Looe Island which is about one mile off the coast…

The Towns and Villages of Cornwall

Lostwithiel

Lostwithiel is a market town on the River Fowey and was once the capital of Cornwall. The town has a long history of being involved in the Cornish tin trade. The Masonic Hall in the town was the Exchequer where tin was weighed and valued and you can still see the remains of a Stannary Court in the Duchy House. Originally the tin from the mines around Lostwithiel left on ships, but after the river silted up the tin was taken by smaller boats down river to Fowey. Later iron was mined and taken down the river on barges. During the English Civil War Lostwithiel was a Parliamentary stronghold, but after being besieged by the Royalist forces in 1644 the town was badly damaged so most buildings here date from after that time…

The Towns and Villages of Cornwall

Lostwithiel

In Lostwithiel it is worth walking around the town when you visit to see the medieval bridge over the river, the old Town Gaol, St Bartholomew's church, and the 18th century Guildhall, once the Corn Exchange, below which is a small local history museum, open April to September. Other local attractions to see include Restormel Castle, located north of Lostwithiel, which you can easily walk to along the river bank. There is a range of retailers in the town, and also quite a few antique shops and auction rooms to browse in whilst you are there…

The Towns and Villages of Cornwall

Mevagissey

Mevagissey has an inner and an outer harbour and is a small village that was once famous for smuggling, but it is now a picturesque seaside resort and fishing port which is popular during the holiday season. The harbour once had a thriving fishing fleet catching pilchards, but today the fleet is much smaller and some of the boats run day fishing trips. You can catch the ferry across to Fowey in the summer months which takes about 35 minutes. The narrow, and sometimes steep, streets and small shops are a delight to browse in. So many happy hours can be spent in Mevagissey…

The Towns and Villages of Cornwall

Mevagissey

A rather odd fact is that the village has a power station run on pilchard oil. The Old Boathouse in Mevagissey now has a museum. If you are here in late July or very early August you can enjoy the annual Mevagissey Feast Week. Take a walk to Dodman Point to enjoy the scenery and be away from the holiday crowds. The main beach is just north at Pentewan and a path takes you there from Mevagissey along an old railway track. Andrew Pears, who created 'Pears' Soap, was born here in 1768…

The Towns and Villages of Cornwall

Morwenstow

Morwenstow is a small village just inside Cornwall near the Devon border and was once the base for the infamous 'wreckers' who lured ships onto the rocks to plunder their cargos. The churchyard of the Norman church has a ship's figurehead marking the burial place of nine men from the "Caledonia" which sunk near here in 1842 AD. The vicar at that time was the Reverend R.S. Hawker, 1803 AD - 1875 AD, a poet who invented the custom of celebrating Harvest Festival. There is good access to several small coves from the village. There is a National Trust car park, toilets and a cafe at nearby Sandy Mouth, and you can walk from here along the cliffs to Duckpool, just one of the lovely coastal walks in the area along the South West Coast Path of Cornwall…

The Towns and Villages of Cornwall

Mousehole harbour and a Cornish cutter

Mousehole

Mousehole is a busy, busy, place in summer as it is one of the most seen fishing villages in Cornwall. It's very pretty, Dylan Thomas called it the '*loveliest village in England*'. Susie and I have holidayed here in the past and would love to go back again some-time soon. The granite houses in the very narrow streets surround the harbour with its small fishing fleet. There is a small beach, with the sands exposed at low tide. The village has numerous small shops. Mousehole is renowned for the Christmas lights display that is held here every year with people coming from far and wide to see the harbour all lit up…

The Towns and Villages of Cornwall

Mousehole

The people of Mousehole holds what they call Tom Bawcock's Eve just before Christmas on the 23rd of December every year. This celebrates the local hero who saved the village from starvation by braving a storm to go fishing. Every year 'Stargazey Pie', fish and potato pie is baked to remember the event. The Spanish burnt the village down in 1595, but left the inn, the Keigwin, intact. That building, although now a private home, still stands today. Mousehole is a favourite scene to paint, both for local and visiting artists. Just offshore is the small and rocky St Clement's Isle. Mousehole is pronounced locally as Mowzzell…

The Towns and Villages of Cornwall

Mullion

Mullion itself is a small village on the Lizard Peninsula, just inland from the famous Mullion Cove. There are shops here, including cafes and art galleries. You might like to take a look at the local parish church, St Mellanus', which has an unusual dog door. Driving down to see the lovely Mullion Cove is a must, and the small local harbour is still used by local fisherman. You get good views if you take a walk along the cliffs, it is well worth making the effort. Whilst Mullion cove is close to the village, the nearest cove is actually Polurrian Cove, which has a hotel. From there you can take the coastal footpath to Mullion Cove and on further to Predannack Heath. The village is close to the famous St Mullion golf course…

The Towns and Villages of Cornwall

Newlyn

Newlyn is a busy working fishing port surrounded by steep hills that rise up from the harbour into the town. Fishing is still very much a part of town life, with a bustling Fish Market and an annual Fish Festival on August Bank Holiday. The town was one of many along this part of the Cornish coast that was attacked by the Spanish in the 16th century. The whole town was burn down, so most of the buildings you see today when you visit date from after that time. Newlyn is very famous for its artists in the late 19th century who made the town well known. Collectively they are known as the Newlyn School of Artists and included Stanhope Forbes and his wife Elizabeth, Walter Langley, T.C.Gotch, and others, many of them trained in France…

The Towns and Villages of Cornwall

All tied up…

Newlyn

The artwork of the Newlyn artist's are on display locally although you have to pop over to the Penlee House Museum in Penzance to see their works, there is still an art society here whose pictures are displayed in exhibitions held at the Newlyn Art Gallery close to the sea front in Newlyn. Most of the local shops are to be found in the Strand, which runs down to the harbour. To the south of the harbour is the parish church, St Peter's, which has the St. Francis Chapel containing the famous 'red dust' which was taken from the Tomb of St. Francis of Assisi. A pleasant little Cornish town to visit or stay in, just next door to Penzance and just before Mousehole. Susie and I passed through it when we stayed at Mousehole and even stayed there ourselves for a week's holiday several years ago…

The Towns and Villages of Cornwall

Newquay

Newquay is a holiday beach resort town on the Cornish north coast, facing the Atlantic Ocean. It's the place to be in the summer and famous for its surfing, so expect to see lots of young people visiting in the summer months. Newquay has a number of beaches, 11 in fact, and has over seven miles of sand. The main beach to the west is the famous Fistral Beach which attracts surfers from all over the world. The other beaches are to the east of the harbour. At low tide the harbour is sandy and is popular with families as it is more sheltered, and close to the town centre. Try Towan Beach for a less breezy beach with rock pools, or out to Watergate Bay. Further afield Mawgan Porth beach is popular. The beaches closer to the town centre have more facilities, the beaches further away are more un-spoilt…

The Towns and Villages of Cornwall

Newquay

Newquay began as a fishing port, the boats here catching pilchards, but during the Industrial Revolution this soon gave way to exporting Cornish tin, china clay, and lead. It was the arrival of the railway that turned the town into this famous resort, originally used to transport goods to the port a passenger service was introduced in 1876, with the train station close to the town centre. The town shopping area is mainly around Bank Street, which is partly pedestrianised, with a mix of chain stores and local shops. Newquay also has the major supermarkets, and out on Chester Road there is an indoor market in a 1930's Art Deco building…

The Towns and Villages of Cornwall

Newquay

In Newquay it is worth taking the time to have a wander around the town and discover its history by taking the 'Newquay Discovery Trail', marked by Cornish slate disks in the pavement. You can also walk over the headland, Towan Head, to see the building known as 'Huers Hu' used to call the fishermen to sea. There's plenty to do, the amusement park, and zoo at Trenance Gardens are only part of what's on offer in this lively resort, and I do mean lively, with clubs and pubs and a great choice of restaurants and other places to eat…

The Towns and Villages of Cornwall

Newquay

Try visiting the west of Newquay where you will find the beaches at Porth and Holywell Bay, as well as Fistral Beach for surfing schools. Why not have a go yourself. Events in Newquay include gig racing using the traditional Cornish boats, and an annual Newquay Fish Festival in early September. The nearest airport is Newquay airport, formerly RAF St Mawgan, which has flights to various UK destinations that include London Gatwick and the Isles of Scilly, and has become more important since Plymouth airport closed…

The Towns and Villages of Cornwall

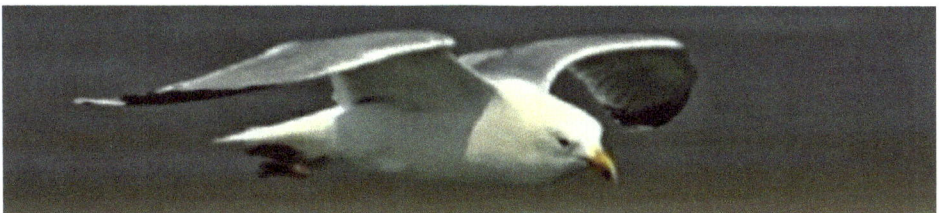

Padstow

Padstow is on the Camel estuary, which is wide here, as it reaches the sea. The old Padstow harbour is a working port even today and you can see the trawlers in the inner dock. It is said that the sheltered harbour once silted up because a local man shot a mermaid with an arrow. In the town the small steep streets rise up into the surrounding hills. Padstow is a good place to visit, but it can get very busy indeed in the summer…

The Towns and Villages of Cornwall

Padstow

Padstow, over recent years, has become a centre for good food. Rick Stein's fish restaurant is in the town, but you need to book in advance. Susie and I have enjoyed very much watching Rick's TV food programs featuring amongst others France, The Mediterranean, India and Venice to Istanbul to name but a few. Susie has most of his cookbooks and so we get to sample many of his recipes quite often. Rick Stein also has a guest house, fish shop, and a fish and chip shop in Padstow. More recent foody newcomers include Paul Ainsworth with his No.6 restaurant…

The Towns and Villages of Cornwall

Padstow

The main car parks in Padstow are along by the harbour and the banks of the estuary. It's worth taking a walk around the town which has mainly small shops, and you can see the 16th Century Raleigh Court on the quay which is where St Walter Raleigh held court. The major event in Padstow is on May Day when the annual Hobby-Horse (*Obby Oss*) dance is held on the 1st May, unless it's a Sunday in which case the event is held on the 2nd of May. Expect lots of music and colour in the streets as everyone enjoys themselves dancing through the streets. It's a popular event with tens of thousands of people attending, so parking is rather difficult and the hotels and bed and breakfasts get booked up very early…

The Towns and Villages of Cornwall

Padstow

Other events in Padstow include the popular Padstow Christmas Festival, and the controversial (to outsiders) Mummers' Day on Boxing Day and New Year's Day when locals blacken their faces to disguise themselves, it is a traditional pagan winter event. If you want to go across the estuary and visit the beaches at Rock there is a pedestrian ferry. Fishing trips and boat trips are also available from the harbour area, which are a delightful way to see the river. Padstow did have a railway station, but that closed in 1967, and the route is now a popular trail that stretches inland towards Wadebridge, and makes an ideal day out walking or on a bike ride…

The Towns and Villages of Cornwall

Marty…

Penryn

Penryn is a large Cornish village on the hill overlooking the estuary of the Penryn River, just outside Falmouth. The town is one of the oldest in Cornwall, with a charter that was granted in 1236 AD. Not long afterwards Glasney College, a religious college, was formed by the Bishop of Exeter. Glasney was demolished after the Dissolution of the Monasteries. The sheltered river port here was once thriving, exporting granite, copper and tin as well as fish. As nearby Falmouth grew Penryn's trade declined. The town makes a good centre for tourists visiting this area…

The Towns and Villages of Cornwall

Penryn

In Penryn there are local shops and if you are in the town you will see buildings from the Tudor, Jacobean and Georgian eras. Local attractions include the small museum in the Town Hall, a granite building that has a clock tower, where you can learn more about Penryn's past. You can easily walk into nearby Falmouth by following the river bank, past the inlets and pleasure boats, as it is very close. More recently a new campus has been built on the outskirts of Penryn to house Falmouth University and parts of the University of Exeter…

The Towns and Villages of Cornwall

Following the catch…

Penzance

Penzance sits in Mount Bay, with small coastal Cornish villages within a short drive that are popular with visitors in the summer. Susie and I spent a pleasant day shopping in Penzance when we were staying in Mousehole. Penzance is the most westerly town in England, and the mildest, creating ideal conditions for sub-tropical plants as evident in the lovely gardens such as the town's Morab Gardens, next to Georgian and Regency terraces. You could also visit St Anthonys Gardens that has an art-deco Open Air Bathing Pool nearby which opened in 1935. There is a large harbour at Penzance together with a busy shipyard and dry dock. It's very much a working harbour with ships and fishing boats as well as pleasure craft. A ferry links Penzance to the Isles of Scilly…

The Towns and Villages of Cornwall

Penzance

In the past you could take a helicopter from Penzance Heliport, but this was closed and the site sold for a supermarket. The nearest flights to the Isles of Scilly are now from Newquay Airport and Exeter Airport, or you can go to Land's End Airport, about 10 miles away. There is a bus service from Penzance railway station to Land's End Airport. The Isles of Scilly are well worth the trip, even if you just go for the day, it takes just over 2 hours by sea to travel the 28 miles. Penzance is an old market town, getting a Royal Charter in 1592 AD, and it has grown into a regional centre for this part of Cornwall. Penzance has close links to the Cornish mining industry, and once had the largest tin smelter in Cornwall. The main town growth came with the arrival of the railway in 1852 AD. Direct trains from London started in 1867 AD, bringing with it tourists keen to take advantage of the milder climate and clean air…

The Towns and Villages of Cornwall

Jack…

Penzance

If, like us, you are wandering around the town when you visit, Chapel Street has historical houses including the Egyptian House as well as the Turks Head Inn, which maybe the oldest pub in Penzance. Most of the shops are nearby in Market Jew Street, where there are small local shops as well as the larger retail chains, and you can also visit the Wharfside Shopping Centre. We really enjoyed our time wandering around the shops in Penzance. A statue of the town's famous son, Humphrey Davey, the miner's safety lamp inventor, stands near the Market House, now a bank…

The Towns and Villages of Cornwall

Penzance

The town of Penzance has a Promenade along the coast and you can walk along it to visit Newlyn, about a mile away westwards. Susie and I walked from Mousehole along the coast path and enjoyed it very much. The Bay sweeps around to St Michaels Mount, possibly part of King Arthurs lost land of Lyonesse. The Mount itself has an 11th century monastery and a 15th century fort. A similar Mount can be found across the English Channel in France. Local beaches can be found in Mount Bay just east of the harbour. The sands extend all the way down to Marazion. For evening entertainment there are a number of night clubs, a 3-screen cinema, and performances at the Acorn Theatre. There's plenty to see and do if you come to Penzance on a holiday or on a short break…

The Towns and Villages of Cornwall

Star of the beach…

Perranporth

Perranporth is one of the best places to go on holiday in Cornwall. Perranporth is famous for its 3 miles of flat sandy beach that attract thousands of visitors each year. Popular with just about everyone, including families as the water is shallow and there are lifeguards here in the summer. Surfers are attracted here as Perran Beach faces out into the Atlantic. The small village of Perranporth, just inland, has local shops and cafes, as well as pubs and other places to eat. You will also find the small Perranzabuloe Museum here that is open from April to October…

The Towns and Villages of Cornwall

Perranporth

Perranporth is named after the local parish, the museum has exhibits on the history of Perranporth and the surrounding area. St Piran, the patron saint of Cornwall, built a church here in the 6th century, but as sand covered over the church a new one was built, but that got eventually covered over as well. The church was dug out in 1835 AD, exposing three headless skeletons! It can be reached from the footpath across the dunes, just north of the town. A popular place to stay, not just for the beach, but as a stop on the South West Coast path that runs through here, so Perranporth is ideal for long walks, or shorter ones amongst the sand dunes that stretch inland from the coast. The author Winston Graham lived in the area, and the scenery here inspired his popular *Poldark* series of books…

The Towns and Villages of Cornwall

The night owl…

Polperro

Polperro is one of Cornwall's most famous, and popular, small fishing villages. The picturesque village with its small and very narrow streets seems to tumble down the hillside to the sea. The River Pol runs through the village. The harbour here still has a small fishing fleet, and is where you can take a boat trip. In the past the fishing fleet was much bigger with pilchards being the main catch. In the 18th century the village's main trade was smuggling, much of which was down to one Zephaniah Job, who controlled most of the smuggling operations. The smuggling was caused by the high taxes on spirits and tobacco. As the streets of Polperro are so narrow you need to park at the top and walk down, although a shuttle bus service runs in the summer…

The Towns and Villages of Cornwall

Flying over bluebells…

Polperro

Most visitors to Polperro come on day trips, so the evenings are quite quiet and peaceful. There are some holiday cottages here, but not many, and they get booked up early, as does self-catering accommodation further inland. The dramatic rugged coastline nearby has a natural pool, which can be used for swimming, but for family beaches you need to go to Looe. There are good walks along the coastal path, it's about 5 miles along the path to Looe from Polperro. Being so pretty it attracts artists painting as they have done for centuries. It's a pleasant place, and there are small shops, places to eat, and you can visit the Polperro Heritage Museum to find out more about the villages history…

The Towns and Villages of Cornwall

Just gliding along…

Polzeath

Polzeath with its twin village, New Polzeath, is on the headland at Hayle Bay opposite Padstow. The village is only small, but does have some shops and places to eat. Its main attraction is the beach which, when the tide is out, is very wide and deep. Lifeguards are here in the summer months. Polzeath makes a good base for touring the north Cornish coastal area, or for just relaxing on the beach. If you like walking, there are cliff top walks along the coast path. Daymer Bay, which also has a beach, is just south of Polzeath, and can be reached by road or the coastal path. Near Daymer Bay is Trebetherick, where Sir John Betjeman, who used to visit the area frequently, is buried at St Enodoc Church…

The Towns and Villages of Cornwall

Happy feet…

Port Isaac

Port Isaac is a small Cornish village, with a little harbour, crammed up against the North Cornish cliffs. It is very popular with the tourists that come here each summer as it is very pretty place to visit. They are a bit strict on parking here, so be careful where you park. The harbour was used as a car park at low tide in the summer, but this was closed as if you were late back your car would be out at sea! Now there are two car parks on the outskirts and a newer one by the school, from all of them you need to walk into the village. The harbour here was a port, established in Tudor times, taking out coal, ores, and other cargoes to larger ships awaiting offshore…

The Towns and Villages of Cornwall

On the lookout…

Port Isaac

In Port Isaac today, there is still a local fishing fleet catching crab and lobster. In the village there are 18th and 19th century cottages, with over 90 listed buildings in the compact centre of Port Isaac's which is a Conservation Area. One place to go is a famous narrow alley called Squeezy Belly, if you are too fat you won't get through! The Fisherman's Friends, who sing old sea shanties, are based here and they can be often found performing in the summer at The Platt down by the harbour. Another famous resident of Port Isaac is the interior designer Laurence Llewelyn-Bowen…

The Towns and Villages of Cornwall

Hide and seek…

Porthcurno

Porthcurno is on the tip of England, just a few miles from Land's End. The small village was made famous as sailors pushed Logan Rock on Tretyn Dinas headland into the sea in 1824, but the locals made them put it back!, the 80 ton granite rock is now balanced on the headland and can be found about a 30 minute walk away from Porthcurno. When you visit, park at the car park and walk down 'The Valley' to the superb beach in a lovely setting, one of the nicest in Cornwall. Porthcurno beach is also famous as the site of the first transatlantic telephone cables to have reached England here from America, although there were earlier cables here across to France. Today you can visit the Porthcurno Telegraph Museum which has recently been re-developed by the trust that owns it and now boasts a cafe which is open to all. This is an ideal place for coastal walks, in either direction, and just nearby to the west is the famous Minack Theatre…

The Towns and Villages of Cornwall

Hare in the long grass…

Porthleven

Porthleven is a small village on the south Cornish coast with a working harbour. Porthleven became important when the Loe Bar sandbank formed, cutting off Helston from the sea. The harbour dates back to the Napoleonic Wars and French prisoners helped to build it. The local Ship Inn is said to be haunted by a ghost of one of the prisoners. Although it had once had a thriving fishing port and boat building was important, the port slowly declined in the early 20th century. The quiet village is located around the harbour with small fisherman cottages, and is worth a wander around. A place for those who like the outdoors, as there are good stretches of beaches suitable for families along the Loe Bar to the east, the nearest one is Porthleven beach. In the westward direction there are cliff top walks and small coves to explore…

The Towns and Villages of Cornwall

In the deep mid-winter

Porthleven

In the winter, Porthleven is well known for the dramatic sea waves that can be as high as 30 feet, crashing against the harbour walls (see above). The winter weather has been responsible for quite a few shipwrecks over the centuries, including that of HMS Anson in 1807 which led to the harbour being built. Out and about, Porthleven is near the National Trust's Penrose Estate and you can take fishing trips from the harbour. Famous people born here include Guy Gibson who commanded the famous 'Dambusters' raid…

The Towns and Villages of Cornwall

Sunshine boy…

Portreath

Portreath is a very small port on the North Cornwall coast, with sandy beaches and rock pools to enjoy. The small village is very popular in the summer, especially with surfers, who take advantage of the waves coming into the two beaches here. The village has a few local shops and pubs. The main car park is down by the harbour. The harbour was built in 1749 AD, replacing an earlier quay that was washed away. As well as fishing, Portreath harbour was used to transport copper to South Wales, the ships returning with coal to power the steam engines used in the mines…

The Towns and Villages of Cornwall

Horse in the long grass

Portreath

In Portreath years ago, getting the goods out of the harbour, was difficult so horse-drawn trams were used until they were replaced by a steam engine winding the trams up the incline to the nearby railway station. Today these old tram lines, and the nearby old railway lines, are used as part of the 'Mineral Tramways Coast to Coast' cycle and walking path. Portreath is a great place for walkers, who can not only explore the coastline but also visit the nearby 250 acre Tehidy Country Park in a lovely wooded valley complete with nature trails…

The Towns and Villages of Cornwall

The beautiful Kingfisher

Redruth

Redruth is a small market town, but was once a very prosperous mining town at the heart of the 18th century Cornish copper industry. The prosperity resulted in the construction of many public buildings in the 19th century as well as religious buildings that included a Wesleyan Church and Quaker Meeting House. When the mining industry declined, so did Redruth, with many miners leaving to go and start a new life in America…

The Towns and Villages of Cornwall

Bringing home the catch

Redruth

Today Redruth is mainly residential, but the historic buildings still remain so if you visit it's worth taking a look around. The Italianate-style Free Methodist Church, the Mining Exchange, used to trade tin and copper, the Victorian theatre, the old Town Hall, and the Clock Tower are just some of the buildings to see. Spot the bronze sculpture of a Cornish miner, erected in 2008, which was designed by the artist David Annand. The shops are clustered around Fore Street, the adjacent Bond Street and Green Lane…

The Towns and Villages of Cornwall

Harry…

Redruth

William Murdock, a Redruth inventor, had the first house in the world that was gas-lit using coal gas. His house, Murdoch House, has been restored. Just to the south-west of Redruth is Carn Brea, a hill with a Neolithic hill fort. It's easy to spot as it has an 1836 AD monument and an unusual 18th century folly designed like a castle. Both were built by a wealthy family, the Bassett family. Famous people who were born in Redruth include the actress Kristin Scott Thomas and Mick Fleetwood, of Fleetwood Mac fame…

The Towns and Villages of Cornwall

Rainbow boy!

Saltash

Saltash is the 'gateway to Cornwall', is the first (or last!) town in Cornwall located on the west bank of the Tamar River, opposite Plymouth. The town is just across from the famous, and impressive, Royal Albert Bridge, built by Brunel in 1859 AD to carry the railway, and the Tamar Road Bridge. On a major road route, the town is now a suburb of Plymouth, having grown considerably over the years into a town of about 15,000 people…

The Towns and Villages of Cornwall

Fawn in the long grass

Saltash

The Saltash shopping area in town is a mix of chain stores and independent shops together with restaurants and pubs. The riverside area is called 'The Waterside' and a visit here gives you views of the estuary and the bridges. You can also get a ferry from the pier across to Plymouth, and in the summer there are boat trips to enjoy. Whilst the town is fairly large it is only a short journey to the south coast as well as to the surrounding countryside. When you visit Saltash there are some historical building of note including the Guildhall and Mary Newman's Cottage, which was the home of Sir Francis Drake's first wife…

The Towns and Villages of Cornwall

St Agnes

St Agnes is a small village just inland from the North Cornish coast. From the Middle Ages the area has been mined for copper, tin and arsenic. Today the old mining workings can still be seen, with ruined engine houses and chimneys dotting the landscape along the cliff tops. The old mines are also still in evidence along the cliff tops and on the headland, St Agnes Head. Today the whole area is designated an Area of Outstanding Natural Beauty and you can walk over the cliffs on the footpath. The nearest beach is at Trevaunance Cove, just a short drive down from St Agnes, there is a car park at the bottom…

The Towns and Villages of Cornwall

St Agnes

Near St Agnes is Trevaunance Cove which was a busy port exporting the ore that was mined locally, but the harbour was swept away by the seas by a storm in 1915. The beach here is popular, but you can also find other beaches nearby, including ones at Chapel Porth and Perranporth. St Agnes has a small collection of shops, cafes, and art galleries to browse in and there is an interesting row of houses on Town Hill, known locally as *Stippy-Stappy.* It's a popular place for tourists to visit, many having a day out on the beach or walking the cliff tops to take in the views. You can also walk up to St Agnes Beacon, just to the west of the village…

The Towns and Villages of Cornwall

A foxy tail…

St Austell

St Austell is one of Cornwall's largest towns and the local area is a major source of China Clay which is exported all over the world. So don't be surprised to see spoil heaps shaped like little white-mountains, and clay pits. China clay, or Kao-Lin, was discovered by William Cookworthy in the 18th century and it is used in the production of porcelain, medicines, and paper. It is said that the china clay pits have no bottom, probably not true but that gives some idea of the size of the pits. St Austell's history is reflected in its buildings, and John Hoge, inventor of the fire engine was born here. Market House, built 1791 AD, and the Holy Trinity church, as well as the Quaker Meeting Room, built in 1829 AD, are some of the old buildings in the town that you can see when you visit…

The Towns and Villages of Cornwall

On the post…

St Austell

When in St Austell see if you can find the flat stone called *The Menagew Stone* in Fore Street. In the town there are plenty of shops, mainly in the more recently developed White River Place, which is a pedestrian precinct. There is a cinema, ten pin bowling, and other things to do in the evening. Don't forget to visit Charlestown, and the Eden Project is very close, only 7 miles away. You can take the bus to get to the Eden Project from the bus station, which is right next to the railway station, or walk there along the old mineral tram route. One other local attraction is, of course, the St Austell Brewery…

The Towns and Villages of Cornwall

Poppy day…

St Cleer

St Cleer is a small village which, with its near neighbour to the west, St Neot, is tucked away on the south side of Bodmin moor. Historically it was a miner's village. Walks might past through St Cleer's when they go for a walk on the moor, but the church here is worth a visit. The church dates from the 13th century. In Well Lane near the church is St. Clarus' holy well. Made of granite it is said to cure madness. Out of St Cleer, towards Redgate you will see two granite cross bases, known as King Donierts Stone. Other attractions nearby include Minions, the highest village in Cornwall, with the Hurlers stone circles and the Rillaton Barrow…

The Towns and Villages of Cornwall

Racing for the line…

St Ives

St Ives is on the north coast of Cornwall and is a popular place for a summer holiday, indeed some visitors come back here year after year. The town does get busy in the summer holiday season, as it is very pretty with cobbled streets and old cottages on the hillside that tumbles down to the harbour. Traditionally St Ives has always been a fishing port with pilchards being the main catch, and a small fleet of trawlers still remain today. The port was where Perkin Warbeck landed in 1497 AD, being proclaimed Richard IV he tried to get to London with his followers but only got as far as Taunton, Somerset…

The Towns and Villages of Cornwall

Out on a limb…

St Ives

Away from St Ives a grassy headland stretches out from the harbour area and on the other side is Porthmeor beach, popular with surfers. The beach has a summer lifeguard. The Tate gallery and the Barbara Hepworth Museum are close to Porthmeor. There are four beaches in St Ives, including the one at the harbour which is exposed at low tide and the family friendly Porthminster beach. The main shopping area is in the streets just above the harbour and has a mix of small local shops and chain stores. Local travel agents arrange day trips in the area and there are boat trips that can be taken from the port…

The Towns and Villages of Cornwall

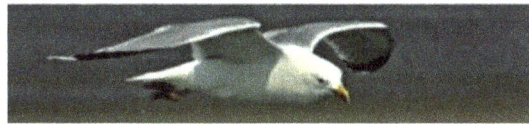

 Hovering!…

St Ives

St Ives is famous for attracting artists such as Bernard Leac, the potter, who came here in the 1920's. Many other artists followed such as Alfred Wallis, Ben Nicholson, Barbara Hepworth and Whistler, many of whom were members of the original St Ives Society of Artists. The town now has a Tate Gallery offshoot situated in a modern purpose built, building. If you are visiting when the lifeboat station, on the quay-side, has its main doors open, you can take a look around the lifeboat and browse in the RNIL shop next door…

The Towns and Villages of Cornwall

In the glad…

St Just

St Just is a small town perched on the cliff top close to Land's End. It is well worth a visit on the way to St Ives on the B3306 as there is dramatic cliff scenery to see all around the area. So get out of the car and get walking and enjoy the views. St Just, is the most westerly town in Great Britain. It has a variety of small shops, places to eat, pubs, and a number of art galleries. So it's worth a wander around. There is a car park here, and a bus service runs from Penzance. Visit the 15th century church to see the wall painting of St George and the Dragon and the Selus Stone inside…

The Towns and Villages of Cornwall

Yellow bloomers…

St Just

In St Just near the church, next to the clock tower, is a medieval amphitheatre, once used for performing local miracle plays. Only one other of this type of amphitheatre, or 'plain-an-gwarries', playing places, survives. It was once a larger town than it is now as it suffered, like many others, when the local mining industry declined. The whole area around St Just is part of the Cornwall and West Devon Mining Landscape World Heritage Site. If you take a walk westwards towards Cape Cornwall you can see an old mine chimney stack and plenty of other evidence of the area's mining heritage. The nearest beaches are at Gwynver and Portherras which are both rocky and small…

The Towns and Villages of Cornwall

Snowy fox…

St Keverne

St Keverne is a small village around a square located just inland from the dramatic coastline in the area near The Lizard. It makes a good base for walking the cliffs and coast along the South West footpath to see the small coves and dramatic sea views. In the village are two public houses, places to eat, and a few shops, that include a Post Office that seems to sell just about everything. The area is famous for two things, shipwrecks and smuggling! The 15th-century church in St Keverne has an octagonal spire and inside is a window dedicated to 106 people who lost their lives when the steamer SS Mohegan went down in 1898 AD in an area just offshore known as the 'Manacles', which has rocks just below the surface of the water. The Manacles has claimed many a life over the centuries. Also in the church graveyard many of the shipwreck victims are buried…

The Towns and Villages of Cornwall

King of the fisherman…

St Keverne

St Keverne also has a unique spot in Cornish history as it was here that, in 1497 AD, the Cornish Rebellion started, an event marked by the statue of the leader, Michael An Gof, in the village. The rebellion began when King Henry VII wanted to raise a war tax, contrary to the long-held rights of the Cornish Stannary Parliament. He marched to London with 15,000 men but were defeated by the King's army and the ringleaders were all hanged. In 1547 AD the local priest, Martin Geoffrey, protested about Edward VI's introduction of the Book of Common Prayer and he was executed in London. More trouble occurred after a mob killed William Body, the King's local representative who was trying to introduce protestant reforms as a result 28 Cornishmen were also executed. However these troubled times are well past, and now St Keverne is a tranquil spot enjoyed by locals and visitors alike…

The Towns and Villages of Cornwall

Stags…

St Mawes

St Mawes is a small Cornish village on the lovely Roseland peninsula next to the River Fal with Falmouth just opposite. It is an old fishing port and the narrow, steep, streets that rise from the port attracts visitors every summer, including yachtsman sailing the area. The village itself has a range of shops, pubs, and places to eat. St Mawes has two good beaches either side of the harbour for relaxing on or taking part in water sports. You can take boat trips from the port as well as using the foot ferry that runs over to Falmouth all year. The St Mawes foot ferry is a nice trip as it passes both St Mawes and Pendennis castles and if you are very lucky you may see dolphins or sharks. The car ferry, King Harry Ferry, is further upstream. It is a chain ferry…

The Towns and Villages of Cornwall

My bleeding heart…

St Mawes

If you are in St Mawes on holiday for a while you can get a *Fal Mussel Card* which gets you a discount on the ferry and other benefits. Henry VIII's St Mawes castle is a good attraction to visit, sited overlooking the estuary, and a visit to St Just in Roseland, a smaller, prettier, village on a creek is worth the time. There are lots of small places to visit, both inland and on the coast, the Roseland peninsula is definitely an area to wander around at a leisurely pace. Of special interest is the gardens here that bloom fabulously in the mild climate. Out and about you could try a trip to Porthscatho, turn off the A3078 just after St Justin-Roseland, to visit this east facing sheltered village with some good beaches nearby. Also worth a look if you are around St Mawes is Portloe, some 5 miles further east, perched on steep cliffs…

The Towns and Villages of Cornwall

Flyby…

The Lizard

The Lizard is a small village close to Lizard Point, the most southerly point of mainland England, with lots of tourist shops, cafes, and a pub. The village has a car park, which is free, and facilities to park coaches. You can walk the half a mile down to Lizard Point, or take the car down the narrow lanes and park at the National Trust car park. Use the cliff top path, but take care as it can be windy. Lizard Point is where the Spanish Armarda was first sighted in the 16th century, and there was a naval sea battle off here in 1707 AD…

The Towns and Villages of Cornwall

Danny and Felix

The Lizard

Today things are rather quieter in The Lizard area and it's a lovely spot to walk along the South West footpath or visit the Heritage centre at the lighthouse. A local ore, serpentine, is dug locally to make into souvenirs which you can buy in the village. The RNLI has a lifeboat stationed just to the east at Kilcobben Cove. Whilst you are in the area Kynance Cove is a nice spot with a cafe in the summer. The cove is to the west, turn right just before you enter Lizard village or walk there from Lizard Point across the cliffs. The whole peninsula is a great place to go to on holiday with the dramatic and rugged cliffs, small coves, and very impressive sea views…

The Towns and Villages of Cornwall

Tintagel

Tintagel is one of the most visited Cornish villages on the north coast. The attraction here is the castle of Tintagel, located high on the cliffs overlooking the sea and rumoured to be the home of King Arthur. The Castle is around a small cove, running over a couple of hill tops. The steep steps and walkways give excellent views. Is it the castle of legend? It was in fact the castle of Reginald Earl of Cornwall in the 12th Century, rather than being the birthplace of King Arthur…

The Towns and Villages of Cornwall

Tintagel

Tintagel Castle is an English Heritage site. The town itself is just one main street, Fore Street, and tourist shops abound which makes it a bit tacky. It's very busy in the summer with the never ending stream of coaches visiting on day-trips. Tintagel does have a Cornish pasty shop, all they sell is pasties, vegie pasties and normal. The pasties are big, but great, buy one to take home. The shop is on the right as you walk towards the castle. The Old Post Office in Tintagel, owned by the National Trust is interesting as it is a small manor house dating from the 14th century. To get away from the crowds, take a walk up onto the headland for the great views down into the village and across the cove…

The Towns and Villages of Cornwall

Gold finch…

Torpoint

The town of Torpoint is now a suburb of Plymouth, which is on the other side of the river. The town is well known for its ferry. The Torpoint Ferry, which is a chain ferry, plies between the town and Plymouth, connecting Cornwall with Devon. The first steam ferries here started in 1834. Torpoint grew as workers from the nearby Devonport Dockyard lived here, but with the decline of the dockland it is more popular with commuters into Plymouth. Being on a headland, there are some nice walks along the banks of the estuary, which gives you the chance to see the boats on the Tamar River. The main attraction near here is Antony House, a National Trust property…

The Towns and Villages of Cornwall

Standing proud…

Truro

Truro is the cathedral city of Cornwall, it was previously a stannery town which was very important for exporting ore. It became a fashionable town in the 18th century and the Georgian buildings remain, these were built by wealthy mine owners. Take a look at Lemon Street, named after Sir William Lemon who was an MP, and Walsingham Place, an early 19th century crescent. It was mining that enabled Truro to grow, and the quayside was always busy. Today, it is a busy county town with a Main Line station. The town operates a park and ride scheme. In the summer you can enjoy a boat trip on the regular service down to Falmouth and St Mawes…

The Towns and Villages of Cornwall

The fruit gatherer…

Truro

Truro Cathedral was built around 1880 on the site of an older church and it is well worth seeing when you visit, as is the Royal Cornwall County Museum to find out more about the city. You also might like to wander in Victoria Gardens. Created in 1898, the gardens are where you can often find a brass band playing on a Sunday afternoon in the summer. If you are here on a Wednesday or Saturday there is a market down at Lemon Quay piazza. The Pannier Market, which has a shopping arcade, is open Monday to Saturday. Truro is a regional centre so there's plenty of shops and places to eat. For evening entertainment there are clubs and bars as well as a four screen cinema and performances at *The Hall for Cornwall,* Cornwall's largest theatre…

The Towns and Villages of Cornwall

High flying…

Wadebridge

Wadebridge has a market, shops in a pedestrianised area, and some industry. The 320 foot bridge over the River Camel, is said to have a base of wool bales to hold the river mud back. Built about 1485, the bridge was widened in 1849 with 17 spans. In the past Wadebridge was a busy river port and more recently a new bridge carries the main road (the A39) just north of Wadebridge bypassing the town. A very popular attraction is the *Camel Trail*, a cycle and walking route along an old railway line. You can take the Trail down to Padstow, about 5 miles away, or you can go inland along the lovely Camel Valley to Bodmin. Near to Wadebridge is the Royal Cornwall Show-ground which hosts the annual Royal Cornwall show. Wadebridge is a pleasant town to visit and there is a footbridge over the river so you can take a walk by the riverside…

The Towns and Villages of Cornwall

The runaway…

Widemouth Bay

Widemouth Bay is a long bay with excellent sand, windswept and dramatic in winter. Located just south of Bude it has ample car parks as the Bay gets busy in the summer as it is a popular surfing beach. It is also quite well-known as the place where communication cables come ashore, there is a GCHQ base just north of Bude. At the south end, just off the beach, are a number of holiday parks, but except for that Widemouth Bay is un-spoilt. Now that we know the location of some of the gardens, castles, towns and villages in Cornwall it is time, in the next chapter to start our exploration of what attractions the county has to offer the visitor…

Exploring Cornwall

Flutter by…

Lands' End

Land's End is as it's name suggest at the southernmost end of England, right at the end of Cornwall. The site is privately owned and is now very commercialised. The nearest village to the attraction is Sennen. The tourist centre at Land's End has gift shops, cafes, exhibitions, audio-visual presentations, play areas, a 4D cinema, and a farm. Of course it has what is probably the famous signpost in the UK, erected in the 1950s showing you how far it is to anywhere, where you can pay to have your photo taken with the signpost showing the place of your choice. Nearly all the attractions have an extra charge. You have to pay for the carpark and you can walk along the cliff paths here for some dramatic views over this part of the Cornish coast. They have a Heritage Trail here now, and you can get a map of the walks at the Visitor Centre. Land's End is, of course, famous as the starting, or finishing, point for many record breaking attempts, by just about all means of transport, to and from John O'Groats in Scotland, complete with a finishing/starting line, depending on which way you went, so you can record your achievement…

Exploring Cornwall

Nuts!...

The Eden Project

Is a living Theatre of Plants in the heart of Cornwall: All life on Earth depends upon the survival of the plants that surround us. Each day of our lives, we use plants from every continent on the planet. The Eden Project is a gateway into this fascinating interactive world of plants and people. A living Theatre, exploring our global garden inheritance and revealing plants, as you've never seen them before. The Eden Project is a truly unique experience, in the heart of Cornwall's Clay Mining country. It is a place where you can explore the amazing relationship that exists between the human population and the fascinating world of plants and the extent that we depend on plants for our very existence…

Exploring Cornwall

Now you see me!…

The Eden Project

Visit the world's largest geodesic domes at The Eden Project. They contain two distinct bio-spheres for you to explore, the Humid Tropical Biome featuring a jungle environment and the Warm Temperate Biome, featuring plant species from the Mediterranean, South Africa and California. Whilst outside there is a series of landscaped gardens where you can enjoy a diverse collection of plants from the Wild Cornwall section to the terraced tea plant slopes…

Exploring Cornwall

The up's and down's…

The Eden Project

The Eden Project is very extensive, requiring a great deal of walking, often up and down sloping terraces. A train runs a regular service from the Visitor Centre to the entrance to the domes, but once inside the biomes there are a number of slopes to be contended with. Comfortable shoes are strongly recommended. Once in the domes, you will immediately notice the change in humidity as you enter the Humid Tropical Biome, where temperatures reach 28° Centigrade. So regardless of the outside temperature, be warned that you will need a top layer of clothing that is easy to take off and carry…

Exploring Cornwall

Mad March Hares...

The Eden Project

On hot days, sun protection is also advisable (sun tan lotion and a hat) as the transparent ETFE film that the biomes are clad in, transmit UV light. To enjoy your visit, plan to spend the whole day as there is so much to see; you need time to enjoy the sites true splendour. A visit to this dramatic and fascinating project will enable you to experience; a fantastic range of plants from around the world. Marvellous stories demonstrating the many ways in which man uses plants for; food, medicine, construction, entertainment, and a whole lot more...

Exploring Cornwall

In flight…

The Eden Project

The Eden Project gives the visitor a glimpse into the future. You will learn about the future use of plants in new designs and technologies. Get a chance to get involved; feeling, tasting, seeing and using plants on themed tours and in a wide range of workshops. Watch demonstrations of the resource used and the showcasing of local and global projects and initiatives that are working towards securing a sustainable future for us all. You will be provided with information and examples of simple practical ideas on how to care for the plants and their habitats. All this to help us all to work towards a sustainable future…

Exploring Cornwall

Tom…

The Minack Theatre

The Minack Theatre is a dramatic open-air theatre set on the Cornish cliffs close to Porthcurno. The unique setting was the dream child of Rowena Cade who personally carried out much of the work to create this inspired place. She toiled for years aided by her gardener and one or two other helpers to create a terrace of seating and a stage above a gully in her cliff-top garden…

Exploring Cornwall

Love is!…

The Merry Maidens

When we were on holiday at Mousehole we venture a little further afield to The Merry Maidens. This is a late Neolithic stone circle located some 3 km from Mousehole in a field close to the B3315, Newlyn-to-Land's End road. It is the best preserved stone circle in Cornwall and consists of nineteen granite stones forming a perfect circle about 24 metres in diameter. The name is said to spring from the cautionary tale that the stones were once a group of frivolous young girls who were petrified for dancing on the Sabbath. In a field close by, a pair of stones are said to be the petrified pipers who played for the dancers. The circle is also known as the Dawn's Men from the Cornish Dans Maen ("Stone Dance"). What curious rituals took place at this and other ancient stone circles will probably never be known. We enjoyed the story anyway…

Exploring Cornwall

Flying the Flag…

Porthcurno Cove

Porthcurno Cove is a sandy cove some 6 km west of Mousehole known mainly from its past history as a telegraph cable station, last used in the late 19th century. Porthcurno's remote beach was selected for the termination of international submarine cables, stretching all the way from Britain to India. This quiet cove was chosen because there was less risk of damage to the cables caused by ships' anchors. The concrete hut on Porthcurno beach, where the incoming cables were connected, is preserved and is now a listed building, and can be visited as part of the Porthcurno Telegraph Museum. About half an hour's walk from the cove can be found the Logan Rock, an 80 tonne granite rocking stone, perched on an outcrop of rock…

Exploring Cornwall

Felix the cat…

Lamorna Cove

Lamorna Cove is located 2 km west of Mousehole and lies in a fertile valley with a pleasant stream. A few cottages and a pub named "The Wink" make up this tiny hamlet. "Wink" refers to the days of smuggling when a wink from the landlord signified that contraband drinks were available at the bar. In the late nineteenth century Lamorna became popular with artists of the Newlyn School. It is particularly associated with the artist Lamorna Birch who lived here and took his name from the place. Others in the colony included Alfred Munnings and Laura and Harold Knight. We walked, one day, from Mousehole to the cove and had a fine old time!…

Exploring Cornwall

Cornish tin mine and Mullion cove

Exploring Cornwall

Prussia and Ready Money coves

Exploring Cornwall

Rinsey beach and Sennen cove

Exploring Cornwall

Rough seas and a Cornish sunset

So now that we know where Mousehole is, some of its rich history and where to go out and about visiting gardens, houses, castles, villages, towns, coves and other visitor attractions in Cornwall it is now time to share with you, in the next chapter, our memories of our own holiday to the wonderful fishing village of Mousehole in beautiful Cornwall…

Our Holiday to Mousehole

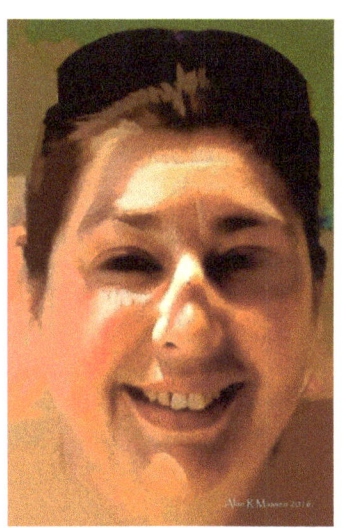

One day in August 2012 my wife Susie surprised me by asking me if I would like a holiday for my birthday present in November of that year? I immediately said **YES** that would be great. But where are you planning on taking me I asked? She reminded me that we had both enjoyed Cornwall when we had been there in the past and she thought that it would be nice to go back there again to celebrate my birthday. I thought that this was a great idea. But where did she want us to stay? Susie went on to explain that this was why she was telling me about her plan beforehand so we could plan it together. We needed to decide where we would like to go, when and what sort of accommodation would suit us the best…

Our Holiday to Mousehole

After giving this some thought, for about five minutes, I suggested we look for somewhere by the beautiful Cornish coast, in a fishing village, in a self-catering apartment that overlooks the sea and a small fishing harbour. We sat still for about thirty seconds and both said together that for us there could only be one place, somewhere where we had been before, that we knew would meet all our needs and that was the small Cornish fishing village of **MOUSEHOLE**...

Our Holiday to Mousehole

Having decided that Mousehole was the place for us it was onto the Internet to search for likely accommodation and dates for our trip. After surfing through various sites we found what we were looking for. We found that in Mousehole overlooking the harbour and sea was a delightful first floor apartment called 'The Sandpiper' which was available for the week that we wanted go. So Susie booked it straight away. Now that we knew when we were going and where we would be staying it was time to plan the transport to get us there and back!…

Our Holiday to Mousehole

Our main problem was that Mousehole is more than 600 miles from our North West Norfolk home and would therefore, not be easy or straight forward to get too. After a discussion we agreed that we had three options in ways to get there. Option one was to drive from ours to Stanstead airport and then to fly from there to Exeter airport then hire a car for the remaining onward part of our journey. We would then have to do the same thing for the return journey. After a short discussion we discounted this option mainly due to the excessive cost it would add to our overall holiday limited budget…

Our Holiday to Mousehole

Lowering the
baulks at Mousehole…

Option two was that we would drive to Downham Market railway station, leave our car there and catch the London train to Kings Cross station. Once there we would then need to take the train from St Pancras station to Penzance station before transferring to Mousehole by local bus or taxi. After some thought, we also discounted this option because of the amount of time it would take to make the journey. It would involve several different types of transport. It would be difficult to co-ordinate timetables to minimise waiting times between stages of the journey. It would mean a reduction in the things we would be able to take with us on holiday because we would have to carry them between trains etc. So all in all the additional cost of the rail tickets, the parking charges, taxi/bus fares and the amount of time it would take to complete our journey we decided to discounted this option as well…

Our Holiday to Mousehole

This left us with just one option which was option three and ultimately the one that we selected. This was that Susie would drive us all the way there in her car. This had the advantage of giving us the use of our own car to get out and about during our stay in Cornwall. It would also mean that we could take more or less whatever we liked with us and not have to carry it. It would be a lot cheaper as we would only have to pay for the fuel we used during our trip there, any excursions we made out and about during our stay and the return journey home…

Our Holiday to Mousehole

Option three it was then but it meant that on the downside of the coin Susie would have to drive all the way there and back, some six plus hours. I could not help her and share the driving because of my poorly knee. I have had a bad left knee for many years (accident at work) and in recent years it has got much worse to the point where I could not drive very far before I was in share agony. I was therefore, not happy to put the responsibility for driving all the way onto Susie shoulders. I felt it was too much for her and suggested that perhaps the train option might be the best one after all…

Our Holiday to Mousehole

Like a flash of lightning Susie, like all good ladies, once again, came up with the solution to our transport problem. She said "why don't we have a stop over-night half way down to Cornwall, say just past Birmingham"? Then in the morning she would be refreshed and we could carry on with our adventure. We could also use the same option on the way back home at the end of the week for the homeward part of our journey. She also pointed out that this would give us an extra day on the front of our holiday, at very little extra cost and it would also add to the adventure. Gleefully I agreed!…

Our Holiday to Mousehole

This decided it was back onto the Internet to find a hotel or motel just off the motorway, just past Birmingham, for us to book. We found a suitable place and pre-booked a room for the night for the outward journey. We decided to see how this worked out and book the return accommodation, should this prove the best solution, for us whilst at Mousehole. Susie said she would bring her laptop so we can do this and also look for places to visit while we are on holiday. So with all these things sorted out, everything booked and the sense of excitement rising all we had to do now was to watch the dates click by until my birthday and the start of our adventure and our re-discovery of the charms of Mousehole in Cornwall…

Our Holiday to Mousehole

When we reached the designated day in November we packed up our car and set off on our great Cornish adventure at 1 pm. Our journey was largely uneventful and so we arrived at our half way accommodation at 4.30 pm. After booking into the hotel we wandered around the area and found somewhere to get something to eat. After a meal and a good night's rest we were up with the lark (7 am) ready to re-commence our journey to Mousehole. We were very excited and the next leg of our journey seemed to take no time at all (3 hours). As we came to the roundabout just outside Penzance we got very excited because we knew that we were only a few more minutes away from our wonderful holiday destination of Mousehole…

Our Holiday to Mousehole

As we rounded the bend that leads into Mousehole and rolled down the hill the wonderful vista of Mousehole harbour opened up before us. We parked the car in the car park that overlooks the sea and walked around the bend into the harbour. Our accommodation the Sandpiper was just on our right and the owner was waiting there to meet and greet us. To gain access to the apartment we had to go down a gap between two shops to the back, and only, door then up some stairs and into the apartment proper. The owners had left us a welcome pack of goodies of some biscuits, bread, jam, milk and a bottle of red wine and very nice they were too. We were very pleased. The apartment was beautiful and was ideal as it had a great view of the harbour and its bobbing up and down fishing boats…

Our Holiday to Mousehole

The Sandpiper Apartment

kitchen and bedroom…

Susie in the lounge.

The Sandpiper apartment in Mousehole

Our Holiday to Mousehole

When we were on holiday in Mousehole for a week in November, at first the harbour was full of boats but by the end of the week it was empty. This was because they lowered wooden baulks across the harbour entrance at the end of the week we were there, to stop winter sea surges damaging the harbour and boats or entering the village itself…

Our Holiday to Mousehole

During the week, they also put up their famous Mousehole Christmas lights display, on and offshore. We sat and watched them do this and while this was going on, the local boat owners took their boats out of the water onto dry land to over winter them. We said that this must make any required boat maintenance work much easier to do. While on holiday I bought a book by Sue Lewington featuring sketches of Mousehole and I used many of her illustrations as inspiration for my Mousehole paintings when I got home. I loved sitting in the harbour and just sketching or watching the birds and locals going about their every day lives…

Our Holiday to Mousehole

The fishing village of Mousehole is perched around its walled harbour on the south coast of Cornwall. We stayed in the right hand building in an apartment called 'The Sandpiper' named after a local sea bird. The apartment was beautiful and its windows overlooked the harbour. We spent many happy hours watching the world go by from our vantage point…

Our Holiday to Mousehole

There are several good restaurants in Mousehole, but by and large we had most of our meals in the pub on the harbour front called the Ship Inn. It was always very busy and I think this was because it over-looks the harbour and people enjoyed sitting at the windows and looking out to sea when it was raining. Like many others I suspect, we preferred to eat there because the food was excellent and the friendly and happy companionship of the locals was even better…

Our Holiday to Mousehole

Mousehole harbour in the early evening…

We did not always eat out and one evening, we even tried the local fish and chip shop, and their fish and chip supper was fantastically fresh, well cooked and very tasty. Other days we would have a breakfast of toasted bread and/or croissants with jam or honey on while sitting at the table that overlooked the harbour in our apartment. I must admit that we took most of our evening meals at the pub or one of the other excellent eating establishment, of which there are many, in Mousehole…

Our Holiday to Mousehole

Red deer…

On our holiday the weather was so good we even managed to sunbathe on the harbour beach on a couple of the days. The locals thought we were quite mad to be on the beach in November in our tee-shirts and shorts, drinking glasses of red wine and sharing a bag of chips from the chip shop. Several came to the railings along the top of the harbour wall and looked down on us with big smiles on their faces. They must have thought 'just look at the crazy tourists'. While sitting on the beach enjoying a glass of wine, some chips or just soaking up the sun we noticed that at the top of the ramp, off the beach, was the local bus stop and village war memorial, and in the picture above we see the local bus waiting to leave the harbour front…

Our Holiday to Mousehole

Most mornings during our holiday, you would find Susie and me sitting with a cup of coffee on the bench on the outside harbour wall balcony overlooking the sea. The Sandpiper studio is behind the first floor windows in the white/yellow house featured in my painting above. It was a very well designed apartment with a kitchen area, lounge and a master bedroom to the back and was fully fitted out with everything the holiday maker needed. There was a car park close by, so we had no problem in getting our luggage to and from the car. The villages and fishermen were very kind and told us that if you wanted fresh bread, you needed to be at the shop on the harbour front by 8.30 am as the shop would be sold out by 9 am. This was true and the bread was worth getting there early as it was very tasty!…

Our Holiday to Mousehole

The Gap…

As already mentioned, to gain access to our apartment in Mousehole, we had to go down a passageway between two shops that we took to calling 'the gap'. It was amazing to come out of the apartment first thing in the morning and walk down this passageway and hear the sounds of a lively harbour gradually getting louder the further you walked down it. We would take a cup of coffee or tea in my case with us and sit on the bench overlooking the harbour and plan our day out while enjoying the sights and sounds of this wonderful place waking up…

Our Holiday to Mousehole

Susie Out and About…

Most days, Susie and I took long walks around the harbour, village and/or into the surrounding countryside. Some of the views we saw were breath-taking and well worth the effort. Some days my knee was very painful so I would stay in the harbour area to just sit and paint, sketch or just watch the world go by while Susie went for a longer walk alone. We ventured away from the village of Mousehole during our holiday and went by local bus to Penzance town, shopping for the day. I think Susie needed this shopping fix because when we were in town she bought herself a lovely black dress in which she looked beautiful. Upon our return to Mousehole, we had a very good fish and chip supper from the local fish and chip shop just two minutes away from our apartment…

Our Holiday to Mousehole

While we were holidaying in Mousehole, I took the time to paint several watercolour paintings. For example, the one at the top of this page, called the 'Mousehole Boy'. The light in Cornwall was very good and I very much enjoyed painting in it. Either looking out of our apartment window or sitting outside by the harbour watching the boats bobbing up and down. We would have our breakfast at the table overlooking the harbour, and then sometimes I would paint if the weather was not kind, but more often than not the sun was shining so we would go out for a walk. When we got back we would often sit on the beach or on the benches that are around the harbour walls and with a glass of wine in hand and watch the world go by…

Our Holiday to Mousehole

Every day of our stay in Mousehole was great. In the village there is so much to see and lots to do that by the end of our holiday we both felt that although we had spent most of our time just wandering or sitting watching the world go by we were totally relaxed and happy. We would encourage anyone who has not yet visited this idyllic spot that they should give it a try, and by way of a change go in December to see the famous Christmas light show in the harbour! In Mousehole there are plenty of tourist shops, fine restaurants, a great pub and a few good galleries, so you are not short of things to do or see in Mousehole or in Cornwall as a whole for that matter any time of the year!…

Our Holiday to Mousehole

As you can imagine we were very sad to be leaving this idyllic spot on the Cornish coast at the end of our week's holiday. I was so pleased and happy with my birthday present and even better Susie was able to share it with me. We both loved it. On our last day we packed up the car at about 8.30 am, tidied the apartment up to leave it as we had found it. We left, wishing everyone that we had met on our holiday all the best and thanked them for all their kindness. They had made our stay such an enjoyable one. After saying our fond farewells we set off back to our Norfolk home. Susie had decided to try and drive the whole way home in one go. She succeeded, and after just two petrol stops, one rest break, one cup of coffee we arrived back in Norfolk some six and a half hour later tired but happy. So to everyone at Mousehole we send a big thank you for having us, and we hope to see you all again real soon…

Our Holiday to Mousehole

In the next and last chapter of this book we will be enjoying some more scenes of Mousehole in Colour but first I would like to say: I was so proud of Susie for driving me all the way home from Mousehole that I thought I would mention just one more time that: On our journey home we fuelled our car up, first in Penzance, then again half way home. We stopped just once for a coffee, to exercise our legs and to have a bite to eat, at our second fuel stop. It took us just over six hours to make the complete journey from Mousehole to our house in Norfolk. Susie was very pleased and relieved to pull onto our driveway. Hopefully, we will manage to go to Mousehole again one day, but as it is a six plus hours car journey for us, which is very tiring for Susie, who has to drive the whole way, due to my poorly knee, maybe, next time it will be by train or even by plane. So until then I leave you with the last few pages of my book that are dedicated to the Cornish Jewel that is Mousehole and it's lovely people!…

Mousehole in Colour

Mousehole in Cornwall

Mousehole in Colour

Mousehole in Cornwall

Mousehole in Colour

Mousehole in Cornwall

Mousehole in Colour

Mousehole in Cornwall

Mousehole in Colour

Mousehole in Cornwall

Mousehole in Colour

Mousehole in Cornwall

Mousehole in Colour

Mousehole in Cornwall

Mousehole in Colour

In the last of the Mousehole in Colour pictures above we see the harbour at sunset, Susie and Alan saying cheers and goodbye from the harbour beach just before we got into our car and left Mousehole behind us and went back home to Norfolk. So until the next time we meet it's goodbye from Susie and it's goodbye from me!…

Acknowledgement

I would like to thank all the people of the Cornish village of Mousehole, that we met on our recent holiday there. They really enriched our stay in this wonderful seaside village and added so much to our Cornish adventure. I would also like to thank my publishers Rainbow Publications UK. For publishing this book and for giving me the opportunity for my books to be read once more. Finally I wish to thank my wife Susie for her love, company and support that she gives me in all that I do every day of my life.

Susie…   **…Alan**

Copyright © 2020 Alan R. Massen

We wish you a fond farewell and a very special

Thank You

www.ingramcontent.com/pod-product-compliance
Lightning Source LLC
Chambersburg PA
CBHW061927290426
44113CB00024B/2837